Flavors of Venice

Flavors of Italy

Rosalba Gioffrè
Gabriella Ganugi

Venice

MᶜRAE BOOKS

Revised edition © 2005

Copyright © McRae Books Srl 2000

ISBN 88-89272-05-8

This book was conceived, edited and designed by
McRae Books Srl, Borgo S. Croce 8, 50122, Florence, Italy
info@mcraebooks.com

Text: Rosalba Gioffrè
Photography: Marco Lanza
Home Economist: Rosalba Gioffrè
Design: Marco Nardi
Layouts: Ornella Fassio, Adriano Nardi, Adina Stefania Dragomir, Sara Mathews
Translation from the Italian: First Edition
Editing: Alison Leach, Anne McRae, Helen Farrell

2 4 6 8 10 9 7 5 3

Color separations: Fotolito Toscana, Florence, Italy
Printed and bound in Italy by D'Auria Industrie Grafiche Spa

Contents

Introduction

The prosperous Veneto region extends eastward from Lake Garda to the Adriatic Sea, and as far south as the estuary of the Po River. The capital city—Venice—is famous and beloved throughout the world, but the whole region harbors a wonderful variety of gastronomic traditions and surprises. The Veneto's remotest origins are shrouded in mystery: a Paleovenetian civilization is thought to have begun between 1500 and 1000 BC when a people of Caucasian origin settled territory between the Alps and the Adriatic Sea. Their civilization reached its high point during the 6th and 5th centuries BC, only to be colonized peacefully by the Romans 400 years later.

From the earliest times, the Veneto acted as a buffer region between the civilizations of Western Europe and Asia. Its contacts with Byzantium were far more important than those with the local Italic tribes. Trade with the East developed early and by the year AD 1000, Venice had become a great maritime power. As a result of this contact, the eating habits and foods of the people with which the city had commercial links gradually spread throughout the region. This was the origin of what is still the essential characteristic of this region's cooking, and which the many culinary traditions of the area have in common: the use of spices. Each province's traditional cooking makes plentiful use not only of pepper but also cloves, cinnamon, and nutmeg, together with such ingredients as golden raisins (sultanas), using them in sweet and savory dishes in a totally unexpected way. Veneto cooking, with its humble ingredients, was transformed by the use of spices into refined gastronomy, with contrasting tastes blending harmoniously with each other in such recipes as *Pollastra in Tecia con funghi* (see recipe, page 61) flavored with cinnamon and cloves, or *Insalata di gallina padovana*

This view of Venice dates from 1600. The city is little changed and many of the same landmarks are still visible today.

Facing page: the domes of San Marco in central Venice.

Below: the island of St. George in the lagoon at Venice.

7

The Rialto Bridge, in Venice. It is worth making a quick visit to the Rialto market near the bridge, where all the typical ingredients of Venetian cooking are to be found, from artichoke hearts to little fish sold ready for frying, and an almost unbelievably varied choice of seafood.

View of the Grand Canal.

(see recipe, page 20), where the chicken is rubbed with freshly ground spices and cooked in a bag.

Polenta or cornmeal, another basic ingredient in Veneto cooking, is a direct descendant of the ancient Romans' *puls*, a porridge made with a mixture of ground cereals that was replaced by corn after the discovery of America. North American corn probably arrived in the Veneto region in the 16th century, imported by the traders of the Serene Republic of Venice who were soon cultivating it themselves. Polenta made with corn had a more appetizing, delicate taste than buckwheat and soon replaced it as a staple food, especially of the poor. The consistency of polenta varies from place to place. It is heavier in the mountains, where it is mixed with butter and served with various cheeses, and lighter near the coast, where it is served with the local *luganega* sausages and soft *sopressa* (a cured meat), or with beans and other vegetables, including *Polenta Fasiolada* (see recipe, page 45), or as an accompaniment to seafood as in *Seppie col Nero* (see recipe, page 80). In Verona it is cooked with wine; on the Adriatic coast slices of polenta are toasted and served with fried fish; in Vicenza very finely ground polenta is used to make a delicious cake, *Pinza Vicentina* (see recipe, page 101).

The Veneto is also rice country. Introduced to the Po delta from the Arab world, rice soon became a key ingredient, especially in the city of Venice. Tender and creamy, rice can be served with everything: in soups, to reinvigorate the body and spirit with warming calories; or as risottos with a wide variety of vegetables, or with any of the seafood caught in the Adriatic sea and the lagoon, and also with meat, as in *Risotto alla Sbirraglia* (see recipe, page 46), and *Riso in Cavroman*, originally a Levantine dish based on a sauce made with mutton. *Risi e Bisi* (see recipe, page 29) is probably the dish most typical of this region with its Eastern influences (a number of similar recipes for rice and peas are to be found in many Greek and Turkish cities around the eastern Adriatic).

Seafarers from time immemorial, the Venetians have exploited the sea to the utmost as a source of food, eating seafood of every conceivable variety, whether fried, poached in fish broth, served in *saor* (sweet and sour sauce), in thick soups, or in casseroles and risottos. Their favorite shellfish are *caparossoli*, the mollusks fished mainly off the coast near Chioggia and the Polesina, where the river flows into the sea and the clam fishers still gather the clams by hand. Then there are *peoci* (mussels), spider crabs, and *schie* (little shrimp), which all end up as *cicchetti* or appetizers (see page 11) on the bars of the local *osterie* or taverns.

Then comes *baccalà* which is actually stockfish (unsalted, dried cod, not salt cod, despite its name) and only here, alone among the regions of Italy, is it transformed into a light, fluffy, and flavorsome mousse, on a par with the most refined haute cuisine. Venetians have the navigator, Piero Querini, who brought it back from the Lofoten Islands, to thank for its discovery; little did he imagine that those stockfish, dried by the winds blowing across northern seas until they were as stiff as boards, would become such an important item in the culinary repertoire of so many Italian regions that the country now imports about 4,000 tons of them a year.

Veneto is a region where people love soups, both light and substantial, and where pasta has never played an important role. The most traditional local pasta, called *bigoli*, are large, wholewheat, rough-textured spaghetti, drawn out with a bronze implement like a wire-drawing tool. Their preparation is traditionally entrusted to men because this dough is so hard to knead manually. *Bigoli* are usually served with *Salsa* (see recipe, page 32), a hot dressing based on onions and anchovies, or with duck (see recipe, page 31), or *Rovinazzi*, a sort of ragù sauce made with chicken giblets.

The daily fish markets in Venice boast an enormous variety of freshly caught local fish and seafood.

The annual *regata storico* (gondola race) is thirsty work. A bottle of local white brings relief to this participant!

Veneto

ITALY

Belluno

Treviso

Vicenza

VENICE

Verona

Padua

ADRIATIC SEA

Rovigo

Venice, the city of the Doges, formerly the magnificent "Serene Republic," lies between the lagoon and the mainland, mistress of the waters of the wide basin on which it is built. Water is without doubt the soul of this place, to which writers such as Goethe and Mann paid homage, and which was immortalized by Canaletto and Francesco Guardi in their paintings. It is from the water that a visitor should take a first look at Venice, gliding in a gondola along the *rii* (small canals), from St. Mark's Square through the city to the Grand Canal, then passing under the Rialto bridge, toward Marco Polo's house, the Malibran theater, the church of Santa Maria dei Miracoli, and the Mercerie. Then slip back through the city and wander along the narrow *calli* (streets), through courtyards and little squares, pausing at several *osterie* for a quick taste of some of their countless *cicchetti* or appetizers made with sardines, *caparossoli* clams, and other fish and shellfish from the lagoon. *Granseola alla Veneziana* (spider crab Venetian-style) is not to be missed, nor is the legendary and unique *Baccalà Mantecato* (see recipe, page 57), the pride and joy of this province's cuisine.

Verona is the second largest city in the Veneto region and one of the richest cities in Italy. Its origins go back to the 1st century BC and its location between Venice and Lombardy has meant that it has always played the role of go-between, not least in matters gastronomic. Starting from Piazza delle Erbe with its multicolored market, you can walk all the way to Piazza dei Signori, where the magnificent Palazzo della Ragione forms the backdrop each year for the end of the San Zeno carnival, with its king, *Papà Gnocco* (Daddy Dumpling) who has a paunch stuffed full of gnocchi, the symbol of Veronese cooking. These gnocchi, usually made with potatoes and flour, were traditionally served with *Pastizzada de caval* (horse meat pie), and are a legacy of Goth and Longbard invaders. Returning by way of Via Cappello, you will come to Juliet's house, still a

In Venice a visit to Florian's Café on St. Mark's Square is almost obligatory, to enjoy a cup of hot chocolate or coffee, surrounded by mirrors and period plasterwork.

Placid and elegant Verona, renowned for its Roman amphitheatre and for being the native city of the ill-starred Shakespearean lovers, Romeo and Juliet, lies spread out between two loops of the River Adige.

Padua is a lovely town to visit, with sights such as the Basilica of St. Anthony and the beautiful medieval squares Piazza delle Erbe and Piazza dei Signori.

Vicenza, "City of Art," is where Palladio's Neoclassical genius found its fullest expression, as witnessed by his marvelous Basilica, the palaces along the Corso Palladio, and this magnificent wooden bridge.

place of pilgrimage for romantics the world over (nearly four thousand letters addressed to the legendary heroine arrive each year). The city is also known for its *Pandoro*, or Christmas cake (see recipe, page 106). *Bollito misto* (a selection of boiled meats) is another specialty and is served with *peará*, a sauce dating from Renaissance times made with bread crumbs, beef marrow, butter, and plenty of black pepper. Isola della Scala, a market town in the lowlands of this province, is the home of Vialone nano, the superb short-grain rice used for risottos. The area's large Valpolicella wine industry is very well represented at Vinitaly, Italy's largest wine fair which is held in Verona each year.

Padua, built on what must once have been an island in the middle of the river, is a lively, busy place. From 1222 onward Padua was one of the major centers of European culture, thanks to its Ateneo (university). It is considered one of the capitals of 14th- and 15th-century Italian art, with frescoes by Giotto in the Scrovegni Chapel, and other works by Donatello and Mantegna. The surrounding area was once home to the legendary (and now unobtainable) Paduan chickens used in a particularly succulent *bollito misto* (selection of boiled meats), and a center for rearing the geese used in traditional Jewish cooking. *Torta Pazientina*, a delicious cake, made with marzipan and zabaglione covered with chocolate, is best savored in the historic Caffè Pedrocchi. The hilly area known as the Berico Euganei produces excellent *prosciutti* (cured hams), whose quality is guaranteed by the Veneto region's *consorzio del prosciutto* (Association of Ham Producers).

Vicenza's gastronomic scene is probably the most varied of the region, from *Baccala alla Vicentina* to *Cappone in Canavera*, not forgetting *Pinza Vicentina*, made with very fine yellow cornmeal, and *Bussolà* (sugar-sprinkled doughnuts). From the surrounding countryside superb vegetables are brought into the city: asparagus from Bassano del

Grappa, peas from Limignano. Asiago's flavorsome cheeses are also worth a mention.

The fertile plain surrounding Treviso, known as the *marca trevigiana*, still merits the poetic description of "the joyous marca." This area is home to the famous radicchio di Treviso, a red endive (chicory) grown in only eight of the province's communes, the product of the experimental flair of a garden designer, Franz Van Den Borre. The variegated Castelfranco radicchio, is an equally tasty and versatile vegetable. Another typical product is *luganega*, a fresh sausage made with pounded pork belly seasoned with pepper and cinnamon, protected as early as the 14th century by an edict of the podestà (a powerful local official) from inferior imitations.

Belluno is situated where the River Piave meets with the much smaller River Ardo and the province is bounded to the north by the alpine area of the Dolomites. Belluno's cooking is based on traditional mountain food, with plenty of game and wild mushrooms, usually accompanied by polenta. Excellent cheeses are made with cow's milk, such as Montasio and schiz, which is fried and eaten with polenta. Delicious red Lamon beans, used in many soups and other dishes, come from this area.

Rovigo is the capital of the province of Polesine. From the early 15th century onward it was a fortified town belonging to the D'Este family. When the River Adigetto was covered in the Fascist era, the city lost its original setting. In the past Rovigo acted as both conduit and melting pot for contacts and cultural trends from Venice and, to an even greater extent, from Ferrara, especially in cooking. *Bisato alla Polesana* (eels served with white polenta) and feathered game dishes, as well as *Tortelli with Misurin* (mallard duck) are all specialties of this area.

A café in Treviso, a pleasant "water town," crisscrossed by canals, washed by the River Sile, and surrounded by lovely rolling hills. Nearby Asolo has spectacular views over the beautiful scenery.

The magnificent Dolomite Mountains make a wonderful backdrop to the city of Belluno.

Antipasti

Venetian cooking is has many recipes for tempting appetizers and snacks. Seafood appetizers are most typical of Venice, where the lagoon and nearby Adriatic offer seafood in abundance. Venetian appetizers are simple dishes, which rely on the high quality and freshness of seafood plucked from the lagoon in the early mornings. These are perfect little offerings to tempt appetites or to accompany a glass of the very fine local wines. Inland, appetizers are more likely to be based upon saor (a sweet and sour sauce).

Zucca marinata
Marinated pumpkin

Peel the pumpkin and remove the seeds and fibrous matter. Cut into slices about ½ in/1 cm thick. ▪ Coat the pumpkin lightly with flour and fry in plenty of very hot oil until golden brown. Drain on paper towels. ▪ Bring the vinegar to a boil in a small saucepan with the garlic and a dash of salt and pepper. ▪ Sprinkle a little salt over the fried pumpkin pieces and arrange in layers in a fairly shallow, straight-sided dish. Sprinkle with pepper and rosemary. ▪ Pour the vinegar over the pumpkin slices, cover with a sheet of plastic wrap (cling film), and leave to marinate for at least 12 hours before serving.

Serves: 6
Preparation: 20 minutes
Cooking: 15 minutes + 12 hours' marinating
Recipe grading: easy

- 2 lb/1 kg pumpkin
- ⅔ cup/100 g all-purpose/plain flour
- olive oil, for frying
- 1 cup/250 ml red wine vinegar
- 1 clove garlic
- 1 sprig fresh rosemary, finely chopped
- salt and freshly ground black pepper

In the past, roasted orangey-yellow pieces of "knobbly skinned pumpkin"
(zucca barucca in Venetian dialect) were sold in the streets of Venice.
Sprinkled with sugar, they were especially popular with children.

Granseola alla veneziana

Crab Venetian-style

Serves: 6
Preparation: about 20 minutes
Cooking: about 7–10 minutes
Recipe grading: easy

- 6 fairly small spider crabs
- juice of 1 lemon
- 2 tablespoons extra-virgin olive oil
- 2 tablespoons finely chopped flat-leaf parsley
- salt and freshly ground white pepper

Suggested wine: a dry, aromatic white (Bianco di Custoza)

Clean the crabs by brushing them with a stiff brush under cold running water, then rinse well. ▪ Cook the crabs for 7–10 minutes in boiling salted water. Insert the tip of a strong knife in the underside, just under the eyes, and lever out the central section of the undershell. Keep the colored, top portions of the shells as "serving dishes." ▪ Take all the flesh out of the shells, discarding the grayish, feathery lungs and reserving the "coral," or eggs. Cut the white flesh into small pieces. ▪ Use special pincers or a nutcracker to break the hard shell of the legs and claws and take out all the flesh. ▪ Combine the lemon juice, oil, parsley, a generous grinding of salt and pepper in a bowl to make a dressing. ▪ Wash and dry the empty shells, then arrange them upside down on a serving dish. Fill with the crab flesh. Top with the coral as a garnish, sprinkle with the dressing, and serve.

The spider crab is the most highly prized of those caught in Venice's saltwater lagoons. It has a very delicate taste which lends itself to this simple preparation. Other types of crab can also be used for this recipe.

Serves: 4–6
Preparation: 20 minutes
Cooking: 5 minutes
Recipe grading: easy

- 2 lb/1 kg medium or large unshelled raw shrimp/prawns
- 2 tablespoons extra-virgin olive oil
- juice of 1 lemon
- 2 tablespoons finely chopped parsley
- salt and freshly ground black pepper

Suggested wine: a light, dry white (Breganze Pinot Bianco)

Canocchie

Shrimp with olive oil and lemon juice

Rinse the shrimp well under cold running water. Bring a large saucepan three-quarters full of salted water to a boil and add all the shrimp at the same time. As soon as the water returns to a boil, drain the shrimp and spread out on a platter until cool. ▪ Use sharp, pointed scissors to snip away the upper shells covering their backs, then discard the shells. Do not remove the heads or tails. ▪ Arrange the shrimp on a large platter. Drizzle with the oil and lemon juice. Sprinkle with the parsley and season with salt and pepper. Serve.

The traditional Venetian recipe calls for mantis shrimp, which is only found in the Adriatic Sea. Its tender, sweet flesh has a very distinctive flavor and this dish is a standard feature in most of the city's best restaurants.

Pesciolini in saor

Sweet sour marinated baby fish

Rinse the fish under cold running water and dry well. Lightly coat with flour. ▪ Heat the oil in a large skillet (frying pan), preferably made of cast iron. When the oil is very hot, add the fish in batches and fry them until they are pale golden brown. Remove with a slotted ladle and spread out to drain on paper towels. Sprinkle with a little salt. ▪ Discard the oil used for frying and pour the olive oil into the same skillet. Add the onions and cook over a moderate heat until they are very tender. ▪ Add the vinegar and a dash of salt and simmer for 10 minutes more. Remove from the heat. ▪ Arrange the fish in layers in a shallow dish, alternating them with the onions. Pour the vinegar over the top. ▪ Cover with plastic wrap (cling film) and leave to stand in a cool place for 2 days before serving.

Serves: 6
Preparation: 30 minutes
Cooking: about 40 minutes
+ 2 days' marinating
Recipe grading: easy

- 2 lb/1 kg baby fish (see below)
- 1⅔ cups/250 g all-purpose/plain flour
- safflower or sunflower seed oil, for frying
- ½ cup/125 ml extra-virgin olive oil
- 1 lb/500 g white onions, thinly sliced
- 2 cups/500 ml red wine vinegar
- salt

Suggested wine: a light, dry white (Soave)

Traditionally, tiny sole, hake, eel, red mullet, and sardines were used in this recipe. Sprats, whitebait, and baby sardines, on their own or together, can be used instead.

Serves: 6
Preparation: 30 minutes
Cooking: about 1 hour
Recipe grading: fairly easy

- 4 lb/2 kg oven-ready free-range chicken or boiling fowl
- ½ onion, thinly sliced
- 1 clove garlic
- 1 stalk celery
- 1 carrot
- 15 black peppercorns
- coarse sea salt
- 4–5 cloves
- 4–5 coriander seeds
- 1 cinnamon stick
- 10–12 cumin seeds
- freshly grated nutmeg
- salt
- about 10 oz/300 g tender young salad greens
- 1½ cups/200 g cooked green/French beans
- 3 tablespoons balsamic vinegar
- 4 tablespoons extra-virgin olive oil
- 30 large, soft white raisins/sultanas
- large piece candied citron peel, cut into matchstick strips
- a suitably sized boiling bag for the chicken (optional)
- a piece of wide, hollow reed (optional)

Suggested wine: a light, dry white
(Colli Berici Chardonnay)

Insalata di gallina padovana

Padua-style chicken salad

Rinse the chicken well inside and out and dry with paper towels. ▪ Stuff the cavity with the onion, garlic, celery, carrot, peppercorns, and a generous dash of coarse sea salt. ▪ Use a mortar and pestle to pound the cloves, coriander seeds, cinnamon, and cumin. Combine with the nutmeg and sprinkle the spices all over the chicken. ▪ If cooking the chicken in a bag, slide it in carefully, head end first, then draw the ends of the bag together around the piece of reed and tie tightly. The hollow reed acts as a chimney to let steam escape during cooking. ▪ Put the chicken in a deep, fairly narrow saucepan into which it will fit snugly, reed or vent end uppermost. Hang the bag from a large skewer placed across the top of the pan. Add sufficient water to cover the chicken; it should not touch the bottom of the pan and the reed should stick out of the water. (Alternatively, boil the chicken very gently, breast uppermost in the usual way.) Add a generous dash of salt and boil gently for about 1 hour. ▪ Take all the flesh off the bones and arrange it on a platter on a bed of the salad greens and French beans. ▪ Prepare a dressing by briefly whisking the balsamic vinegar, oil, and a little of the cooking juices from the boiling bag. ▪ Garnish with the white raisins and citron peel. Drizzle with the dressing and serve.

Cooking the chicken in a bag harks back to the traditional method of boiling it in a pig's bladder with the reed protruding to act as a chimney.

Il cicchetto: Venice's osterie

No self-respecting Venetian fails to find an opportunity sometime during the day to visit the local *cicchetto*, or *osteria* (Venice's traditional eating-places-cum-wine-shops), for a small glass of wine and a chat, or for a quick but tasty meal at lunchtime or before going to the cinema in the evening. In Venice these *osterie* survive even in the face of competition from fast food places selling *panini* and slices of pizza. As traditional eating-houses, they have always been places where people met up with one another at almost any time of day, in a warm and welcoming atmosphere. Predictably, seafood is the most frequent dish on the menu; fishermen were once the osteries' most regular

customers, gathered around the tables, talking noisily and playing cards. Then we come to the wines, often not great ones, but pleasing and fresh tasting wines to chat over. Outside Venice, *osterie* flourish along the old trading routes; and here the choice of *cicchetti* (snacks) is no less varied. You can savor homemade *soppressa* (a very soft type of salami); fried or braised *castraure* (tiny baby artichoke buds); zucchini flowers dipped in batter and fried; baby octopus and vegetables in sweet sour dressing (in *saor*), pig's feet (trotters) with Savoy cabbage; marinated pumpkin; beans with the local dressing, and hard-cooked eggs, all served with refreshing wines and infinite courtesy.

Most *osterie* still have a separate section set aside for meals, as well as unlaid tables (usually near the long bar where the oste or proprietor presides) where regular customers and occasional visitors gather to drink and savor the variety of *cicchetti* (snacks) on offer. In Venice the word *cicchetto* does not mean what it usually does throughout the rest of Italy – a small glass of some alcoholic drink – but, instead, food that accompanies it to enhance the wine's bouquet and satisfy the palate. Arranged on display you will find fried fish, sardines in sweet sour sauce, baby octopus and squid, creamed stockfish with hot toast or polenta slices, firm omelettes or frittatas, and an incredible variety of shellfish, all cooked to perfection.

As you wander along the *calle* (the narrow streets of Venice), keep a look out for these traditional eating and drinking venues. You will be able to taste the best of real Venetian cooking and experience a slice of typical local life. Although there are not many left nowadays, they are relatively easy to find. Some, like the *Codroma*, are historic places. Founded at the beginning of the 20th century, it has kept its original interiors. Then there is Ai do Draghi in Campo Santa Margherita, now mainly frequented by university students. The Cantina do Mori is one of the oldest, with a good selection of wines served at the bar.

Serves: 6
Preparation: 20 minutes
Cooking: 15 minutes
Recipe grading: easy

- 2¼ lb/1.2 kg very fresh small clams
- ½ cup/125 ml extra-virgin olive oil
- 2 cloves garlic, peeled and lightly crushed
- 1 cup/250 ml dry white wine
- 2 tablespoons finely chopped flat-leaf parsley
- freshly ground black pepper

Suggested wine: a dry white
(Breganze Pinot Grigio)

Pevarasse in bianco
Clams cooked in white wine

Scrub the clams free of any seaweed and dirt, then "purge" them (see below). ▪ Drain well and place in a large saucepan with the oil and garlic. Cover tightly and cook over a high heat, shaking the pan from time to time, for just under 10 minutes, or until they have all opened (discard any that do not). ▪ Add the wine, parsley, and a grinding of pepper. Cook for 5 minutes more. ▪ Serve hot.

"Pevarasse" is the Venetian dialect word for little clams which belong to the Veneridae family; from this same family, "caparossoli" are even more highly esteemed throughout the coastal region. Any small clams can be used, but they must be left to stand for a few hours in a large bowl of very cold salted water, changed two or three times, before cooking, so that they release all their sand. This recipe can also be used for mussels.

Serves: 6
Preparation: 30 minutes
Cooking: 20 minutes
Recipe grading: easy

- 10 oz/300 g fresh mushrooms (porcini, or white cultivated mushrooms, or a mixture of the two)
- 4 tablespoons butter
- 1 tablespoon brandy
- scant 1 cup/200 ml light/single cream
- 3½ oz/100 g semi-soft melting cheese (stracchino, robiola, or similar)
- 1 small white truffle, fresh if possible, grated
- 12 slices of French bread, toasted

Suggested wine: a dry red
(Colli Euganei Rosso)

Crostini di funghi al tartufo

Mushroom and truffle toasts

Clean the mushrooms thoroughly and chop them coarsely with a *mezzaluna* (half-moon chopper) or large kitchen knife. ▪ Melt the butter in a skillet (frying pan) and add the mushrooms a few at a time (giving the moisture produced a chance to evaporate). Cook, stirring at intervals, until they are done. ▪ Sprinkle with the brandy and cook until it has evaporated. ▪ Heat the cream separately in a small saucepan. Add the cheese and let it melt over a low heat while stirring. ▪ When the cheese is completely blended with the cream, remove from the heat and stir in the mushrooms and the truffle. ▪ Spread this mixture on the pieces of toast and serve hot.

If fresh truffles are unavailable, truffle paste is a good substitute.

Patè di fegato

Liver pâté

Prepare the liver by following the recipe for "Liver Venetian-Style" on page 60. ▪ Chop the liver mixture very finely, then work it into the butter, beating vigorously with a wooden spoon until the two ingredients are smoothly blended. ▪ Transfer the pâté to a mold and chill in the refrigerator for 2–3 hours before serving.

Serves: 6
Preparation: 20 minutes
+ 2–3 hours' chilling
Recipe grading: easy

- 1¼ lb/625 g calves' liver
- 1¼ lb/625 g white onions
- 2 cups/500 g butter
- ½ cup/125 ml extra-virgin olive oil
- 2 tablespoons finely chopped flat-leaf parsley
- salt and freshly ground black pepper

Suggested wine: a light, dry rosé
(Bardolino Chiaretto)

This very simple and utterly delicious recipe probably originated as a way of using up leftovers of Fegato alla Veneziana – Liver Venetian-Style. *If you line the mold with plastic wrap (cling film), it will be easier to turn out.*

Primi piatti

While there is no shortage of recipes for succulent tagliatelle and other traditional pasta dishes, at heart, Veneto is the land of risottos, soups, and minestre, all with rice as the main ingredient. In this region risottos are normally served all'onda, which means with slightly more liquid than you would normally expect. Polenta, whether it be white or yellow, is another basic ingredient in many first courses: sometimes firm and sometimes almost runny, it is served with a variety of vegetable, meat, and cheese sauces. Next day, when it is cold and firm, it is sliced, fried in olive oil, and served as an appetizer.

Risi e bisi

Rice and peas

Hull (shell) the peas. Set the peas aside and rinse the pods well. Boil the pods for 20–30 minutes in salted water. Drain and push through a fine sieve. ▪ Stir the pea pod purée into the broth in a large saucepan and keep hot. ▪ Set aside one-third of the butter and melt the rest in a heavy-bottomed saucepan. Fry the pancetta and the finely chopped onion in the butter. Add the rice, stir well for 2–3 minutes, and then sprinkle with the wine. ▪ When the wine has evaporated, add the peas, cook for 2–3 minutes, and then add half of the hot broth. ▪ Keep stirring frequently, adding more broth as the liquid is absorbed, until the rice is tender but still has a little bite to it. It should be very moist. ▪ Remove from the heat. ▪ Stir in the remaining butter and the parmesan and season to taste. Sprinkle with the parsley and serve.

Serves: 6
Preparation: about 30 minutes
Cooking: about 50 minutes
Recipe grading: easy

- 2⅓ lb/1.3 kg very fresh, young peas in the pod
- 2 cups/500 ml broth/stock made with a bouillon cube
- 6 tablespoons butter
- ½ cup/60 g diced Italian pancetta or thick slices bacon (streaky bacon)
- 1 onion, finely chopped
- 2½ cups/500 g Italian risotto rice
- ½ cup/125 ml dry white wine
- scant 1 cup/100 g freshly grated parmesan cheese
- salt and freshly ground black pepper
- 2 tablespoons finely chopped parsley

Suggested wine: a light, dry white (Soave Classico)

This dish was traditionally served to the Doge, the ruler of Venice, on April 25, the feast day of St. Mark. It is still very popular in the countries which were once dominated by "La Serenissima," (the city state of Venice), including Greece, Turkey, and Lebanon. The original recipe was flavored with anise seeds.

Bigoli con l'anara
Wholewheat spaghetti with duck

Sift the flour and salt into a mound on a pastry slab or into a large mixing bowl. Make a well in the center and break the eggs into it. Stir with your fingers or a fork, gradually incorporating the flour and adding water a little at a time, as needed; the dough should be smooth and elastic. Cover the bowl with a damp cloth and leave to stand for 30 minutes. • Make the thick spaghetti-shaped bigoli using an electric or hand-cranked pasta machine. (Venetians use a special utensil like a food mill with a disk perforated with fairly large holes. The pasta is extruded through these holes and spread out on a lightly floured board to dry.) • Wash and dry the duck. Place in a large, oval flameproof casserole, then add enough water to cover, a dash of salt, and the onion, celery, and carrot. Bring to a boil and cook gently for 1 hour. • While the duck is cooking, chop the liver and heart coarsely and sauté in the oil and butter over a high heat. When lightly browned, add the sage leaves, salt, and a generous grinding of pepper. • Remove the cooked duck from the casserole and strain the broth. • Cook the pasta in the broth for 5–7 minutes, and drain. Mix in the fried liver, oil and butter, and plenty of parmesan.

Serves: 6
Preparation: 40 minutes
Cooking: 45 minutes + 30 minutes resting
Recipe grading: complicated

For the pasta:
- 2⅔ cups/400 g whole-wheat/wholemeal flour
- salt
- 4 eggs
- 4 tablespoons cold water

For the sauce:
- 1 young duck, with its liver and heart
- 1 onion
- 1 stalk celery
- 1 carrot
- 4 tablespoons extra-virgin olive oil
- 5 tablespoons butter
- 2–3 leaves fresh sage, torn
- salt and freshly ground black pepper
- freshly grated parmesan cheese

Suggested wine: a dry red
(Colli Euganei Cabernet)

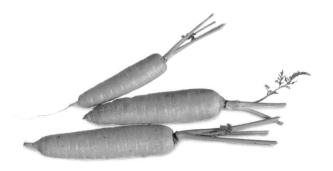

Bigoli look like very fat spaghetti made with wholewheat flour. You can use an electric or hand-cranked pasta machine instead of the traditional "bigolaro" to make them. Other types of fresh or dried wholewheat pasta can be used instead (the dried types will take a little longer to cook).

Bigoli in salsa

Wholewheat spaghetti with onions and anchovies

Serves: 6
Preparation: 30 minutes + 30 minutes
     resting
Cooking: 20 minutes
Recipe grading: fairly easy

- 1 quantity bigoli (wholewheat spaghetti – see recipe, page 31)
- 7 oz/200 g salted anchovies (or sardines)
- scant ½ cup/100 ml extra-virgin olive oil
- 3 large white onions, finely sliced
- 2 tablespoons finely chopped parsley
- salt and freshly ground black pepper

Suggested wine: a dry red
(Colli Berici Cabernet)

This dish was traditionally served on days of abstinence and fasting, such as Christmas Eve, Ash Wednesday, and Good Friday. Nowadays it has become a gourmet dish. For a slightly different dish, add ½ cup/100 g of canned tuna, drained of its oil, at the same time as the anchovies.

Prepare the bigoli and spread them out on a floured board or work surface to dry for about 30 minutes. ▪ Rinse the anchovies thoroughly, remove the bones, and chop the flesh coarsely. ▪ Heat the oil in a large skillet (frying pan) and add the onions. Cook gently until tender, adding a spoonful or two of water, if necessary, to prevent them from browning. ▪ Add the anchovies, then turn up the heat and use a fork or wooden spoon to break them up so that they dissolve in the oil. Season generously with salt and pepper and turn off the heat. ▪ Cook the bigoli in plenty of very lightly salted water for 5–7 minutes. ▪ Drain and stir into the onion, oil, and anchovy mixture. Sprinkle with the parsley and serve.

Panada

Savory bread pudding

Slice the bread and place it in a flameproof casserole or saucepan. Pour in sufficient warm broth to cover it. Sprinkle with the cinnamon and 2 tablespoons of oil, then leave to stand for 40 minutes. ▪ Place over a gentle heat and stir frequently until it turns into a smooth mixture (this will take about 40 minutes). ▪ Add the parmesan and a dash of salt. Stir well, drizzle with the remaining oil, then serve.

Serves: 6
Preparation: 5 minutes + 40 minutes' soaking
Cooking: 40 minutes
Recipe grading: easy

- 1 lb/500 g stale white bread
- 1½ quarts/1.5 liters beef broth/stock, homemade or bouillon cube
- dash of ground cinnamon
- 3 tablespoons extra-virgin olive oil
- 1 cup/125 g freshly grated parmesan cheese
- salt

Suggested wine: a light, dry white (Verduzzo del Piave)

This dish, made with leftover bread, is traditionally served during Lent. Place the casserole, uncovered, in a preheated oven at 400°F/200°C/gas 6 to give it an attractive golden brown crust on top.

33

Serves: 6
Preparation: 1 hour
Cooking: 20 minutes
Recipe grading: complicated

For the pasta:
- 2⅔ cups/500 g unbleached all-purpose/strong plain flour
- 5 eggs
- 2 tablespoons warm water
- salt

For the filling:
- 2 lb/1 kg boiled beets/beetroot
- ¾ cup/180 g butter
- salt
- scant ½ cup/100 g ricotta cheese
- fine bread crumbs (optional)
- 1 tablespoon poppy seeds
- freshly grated parmesan cheese

Suggested wine: a dry, aromatic white
(Lison Pramaggiore Chardonnay)

Casumzieei ampezzani
Ravioli with beet stuffing

Sift the flour onto a pastry board or into a large mixing bowl. Make a well in the center and break the eggs into it. Add the water and salt, and stir with your fingertips or a fork so that the flour is gradually incorporated. Knead the dough with the palms of your hands until it is smooth and elastic. Cover with a damp cloth and leave to rest for about 30 minutes. ▪ Chop the beets and sauté over a high heat in half the butter and a dash of salt. ▪ Remove from the heat, stir in the ricotta, adding some bread crumbs if the stuffing mixture is too moist. ▪ Roll out the pasta dough with a floured rolling pin on a floured board, rolling from the center outward, until the sheet is very thin (⅛ in/3 mm) and of an even thickness. Dust the dough and rolling pin with flour as necessary while you work. ▪ Use the rim of a 3 in/8 cm diameter glass or round cookie cutter to cut out disks from the sheet. ▪ Place a little of the filling in the center of each disk and fold it in half, enclosing the filling. Pinch the edges firmly together with the tips of your fingers to seal well. ▪ Add the ravioli carefully to a large pan of salted, boiling water and cook for about 10 minutes. ▪ Drain well. Transfer to a serving dish, dot with the remaining butter, and sprinkle with the poppy seeds. ▪ Sprinkle with plenty of parmesan cheese and serve.

This is a meatless ravioli, often served during Lent, and a specialty of Cortina d'Ampezzo. Try replacing the ricotta with 3½ oz/100 g boiled, mashed floury potatoes.

The wines of the Veneto

According to an old Venetian saying "he who drinks well, sleeps well; he who sleeps well thinks no evil; he who thinks no evil does no evil; he who does no evil goes to heaven. So drink well and you will go to heaven." The Veneto has long been the home of fine wines and it is still one of the most important wine producing areas in Italy. Wine growing has shaped the geography and economy of this region for centuries.

Bardolino, produced in the area to the south east of Lake Garda, is a ruby or light pink red wine that must be drunk young. It has a fresh, dry taste, suitable for drinking with soups, pasta dishes, white meats and, best of all, with pork products (*salumi*) and unmatured cheeses.

The culture of wine is entwined with the history of the region; the towns grew up in the various wine producing areas around the summer retreats of aristocratic families. Designed by illustrious architects and decorated by famous artists, many of these villas are now the centers of prestigious wine businesses. Between October and February, it is possible to visit some of these historic cellars and the lofts where the grapes are placed to dry on racks before they are pressed. Vineyards now cover about 50,600 acres (125,000 hectares) of land, with wine production totalling nearly 264,000 gallons (7,000,000 hectoliters) in 1997, of which nearly one-third were D.O.C. (government guaranteed) fine wines. After a somewhat inglorious past, when production was geared mainly to quantity, the producers have undergone what could be described as a revolution in recent years, and the main wine-makers strive to achieve a higher average quality, resulting in their labels being synonymous with good value, including those in the ordinary table wine sector.

Soave, made with Garganega and Trebbiano grapes in the area to the east of Verona, is the most well known of the region's white wines. In recent years it has improved greatly, thanks to the producers' newfound commitment to quality. With its delicate bouquet and its dry, fresh, light taste, *Soave* can be served with egg, fish, and poultry dishes.

Valpolicella, produced in the hills to the north of Verona, is probably one of the most well-known wines in the world. The most highly prized red labels are created from Corvina, Rondinella, and Molinara grapes. The best of them all, *Amarone*, has been much sought after since the 1950s, when tastes began to veer in favor of drier wines. To make wines of an intense ruby color, acquiring garnet shades as they age, the grapes are left to dry partially on racks in lofts. After aging in oak casks for three years, the wine is bottled and can then age for as long as 20 years without losing its character. *Amarone*, with its full, pure bouquet and its dry yet soft and velvety taste, goes very well with game, mature cheeses, and Verona's classic dish, braised beef.

Also worthy of mention is *Bianco di Custoza* from the southern shores of Lake Garda. It is made from Trebbiano and Garganega grapes with small amounts of Tokay, Cortese, Riesling, Chardonnay, and Malvasia. It has an intense bouquet and a pleasing, slightly bitter aftertaste.

Around the hamlet of San Piero di Bardozza, in the Valdobbiadene area, covering an area of barely 40 acres (100 hectares), Cartizze grapes are grown. These have a high sugar content and are used to produce a particularly sought after semi-sweet sparkling white wine.

Recioto, known to have already been in production in Pliny the Elder's time, is a full, semi-sweet wine with a hint of wild violets to its bouquet. Its name may be derived from the dialect "*recie*" from *orecchie* (meaning "ears") used to denote the grape bunches uppermost, the sweetest portions of which are selected for this wine. *Recioto* is excellent with all sorts of cookies and also with soft cheese and exotic fruit. The *amandorlata* version which has a subtle almond flavor, goes perfectly with chocolate.

Recioto di Soave, also made with Garganega and Trebbiano grapes, is a dessert wine, or "*vino da meditazione*" as the Italians call it. Still or sparkling, it has a harmonious taste, with a hint of raisins and almonds.

Prosecco, named after its grape variety, is cultivated in the hilly area of Marca Trevigiana. *Prosecco D.O.C* is produced in the Conegliano and Valdobbiadene regions. With its subtle bouquet of acacia, wisteria, and wild honey, it varies from dry to *amabile* (semi-sweet). The still varieties make good table wines, while the sparkling types are more suitable with dessert or as an aperitif. Dry *Prosecco* goes well with risotto and non-oily fish. Semi-sweet *Prosecco* enhances the taste of shellfish, and the sparkling version (*spumante*) is perfect with fruit salad.

Pasticcio di radicchio trevigiano

Treviso radicchio and pasta pie

Rinse the radicchio heads well. Slice them lengthwise into quarters and place in an ovenproof dish lightly greased with the first measure of butter. Season with salt and pepper and pour the cream over the top. ▪ Bake in a preheated oven at 350°F/180°C/gas 4 for 15 minutes. ▪ Make a fairly liquid Béchamel sauce: melt the butter, stir in the flour, then gradually add the boiling milk. Stir continuously to prevent lumps from forming. Cook over a very gentle heat until the sauce has thickened. Add a dash each of salt and nutmeg. ▪ Cook the pasta in a large saucepan of salted, boiling water until al dente (tender but still firm to the bite). This will take about 5 minutes. Drain thoroughly. ▪ Mix the pasta with the radicchio and Béchamel and transfer to an ovenproof dish. Sprinkle with the parmesan and bake in a preheated oven at 400°F/200°C/gas 6 for 20 minutes. ▪ When a golden brown crust has formed on the top, serve piping hot, straight from the ovenproof dish.

Serves: 6
Preparation: 10 minutes
Cooking: 35 minutes
Recipe grading: complicated

- 6 heads of Treviso radicchio
- 2 tablespoons butter
- salt and freshly ground black pepper
- 1¼ cups/310 ml whipping cream

For the Béchamel sauce:
- 4 tablespoons butter
- 4 tablespoons all-purpose/plain flour
- 2 cups/500 ml boiling milk
- salt
- nutmeg

- 14 oz/400 g maltagliati pasta
- scant 1 cup/100 g freshly grated parmesan cheese

Suggested wine: a light, dry white (Soave Classico)

You can use other types of fresh pasta, such as pappardelle *or* tagliatelle, *instead of* maltagliati.

Serves: 6
Preparation: about 40 minutes
Cooking: about 3½ hours
Recipe grading: fairly easy

- 4 oven-ready pigeons, preferably with their livers
- 1 onion, finely chopped
- 1 celery heart, finely chopped
- 1 carrot, finely chopped
- 2 tablespoons extra-virgin olive oil
- ⅔ cup/150 g butter
- 1 cup/250 ml dry white wine
- 2 quarts/2 liters light broth/stock (homemade or bouillon cube)
- 9 large slices of stale bread, not more than ½ in/1 cm thick
- 1¾ cups/215 g freshly grated parmesan cheese
- salt and freshly ground black pepper

Suggested wine: a dry red
(Bardolino Superiore)

Sopa coada

Braised pigeons

Cut the pigeons in half. ▪ Fry the onion, celery heart, and carrot gently in the oil and one-third of the butter for a few minutes. ▪ Place the pigeons, outer, fleshy side down, on top of the chopped vegetables and brown well. ▪ Add the wine and cook until it has evaporated. ▪ Pour in enough broth to cover the birds and season with salt and pepper. Cook over a low heat for about 1 hour. ▪ When the pigeons are done, add their livers (if available) cut into small pieces, and cook for 5 minutes more. Remove from the heat and leave to cool. ▪ Take the flesh off the bones, breaking it up as little as possible. ▪ Grease a deep ovenproof dish with butter, place 3 bread slices in the bottom, and cover with half the pigeon flesh. Sprinkle with some of the cooking liquid and some parmesan. Repeat this process, then cover with a third, final bread layer. Pour more cooking liquid over the top layer and sprinkle with the remaining parmesan. ▪ Cook, uncovered, in a preheated oven at 300°F/150°C/gas 2 for at least 2 hours, basting with a little more broth at intervals, to keep it moist. ▪ Serve hot, accompanied by a cup of broth.

"Coada" is Venetian dialect for covata, *a picturesque way of describing very slow cooking in the oven. This recipe also works very well with chicken; rosemary can be added for extra flavor. There is even a vegetable version made with Savoy cabbage, onions, spinach, and fennel, spiced with mace or nutmeg.* Sopa Coada *is excellent reheated in the oven the day after it is made.*

40

Jewish cooking

It is impossible to tell whether Jewish cooking influenced that of Venice or whether the Jews adopted some of the Venetians' culinary traditions. Venetians undoubtedly welcomed some Jewish practices as novelties and copied the use of certain ingredients and recipes, absorbing these as part of its own traditional cooking which had already been considerably influenced by the cooking of those nations with whom Venice had commercial contacts. Jewish people lived in Venice from the 12th century onward: they were not only traders and bankers, but also moneylenders, an activity which led to such public obloquy that they were expelled from the city some two centuries later. In 1516 they were allowed back into Venice, but confined to a quarter known as the ghetto, where the state foundries or *getti* (metal casting workshops) were sited. With Jewish pronunciation, this word became "ghetto" and was in common use throughout Europe in the 16th century, to denote the compulsory living quarters designated for Jews. The ghetto was a very restricted area enclosed by high gates, to which all Jews had to return at sunset; their dwellings were very small, often inadequate for family needs and thus it was normal for many activities to take place outside. During the 16th century the cultural influence of the Jewish community became very considerable; in 1534 the Jewish university was founded, Jewish doctors were the most sought after, as were Jewish music and singing teachers; the Jews spoke many languages and were therefore employed as interpreters and intermediaries in the households of diplomats and traders.

Padua also had a very important Jewish community. In that city their gastronomic traditions were held in such high esteem that the butcher's shop under the *Palazzo della Ragione* butchered meat according to the dictates of the Talmud. The non-Jewish population used these meats for their own traditional dish, mixed boiled meats. Paduans also adopted Jewish methods of cooking white meats such as chicken or turkey (the local dish of young turkey with pomegranate was a traditional Passover dish, and the Paduan custom of cooking chicken with orange or lemon juice is also of Jewish origin).

Left: Jewish apothecary in Venice during the 16th century.
Opposite (top): The Giudecca, in Venice; (bottom) The Festa del Redentore.

Cheese Frisinsal
For six

1 onion, finely chopped
1 clove garlic, finely chopped
2 tablespoons finely chopped parsley
1 sprig finely chopped fresh rosemary
½ cup/125 ml extra-virgin olive oil
10 oz/300 g mushrooms
salt
7 oz/200 g peas
1 scallion/spring onion or shallot,
   finely chopped
1 packet of puff pastry, pre-rolled
1 lb/500 g ziti pasta, cooked until tender
7 oz/200g freshly grated parmesan cheese
1 egg yolk, beaten with a little milk

Chop the onion very finely with the garlic, parsley, and rosemary leaves and fry gently in most of the oil; add the mushrooms, cut into small pieces. ▪ Season with salt and cook over a low heat for approximately 20 minutes. ▪ Gently fry the peas and the finely chopped scallion in the remaining oil in a separate skillet or small saucepan for approximately 15 minutes; add a pinch of salt just before removing from the heat. Make the puff pastry and use two-thirds of it to line a springform cake pan 10 in/26 cm in diameter. ▪ Mix the cooked, drained pasta with the contents of both skillets (the mushroom and herb mixture and the peas and scallion) and the cheese. ▪ Fill the pastry lined pan with this and level the surface before covering with the remaining pastry, rolled out to form a lid; pinch the edges together to seal firmly, and brush the surface with the egg glaze. ▪ Bake in a preheated oven at 400°F/200°C/gas 6 for approximately 40 minutes and serve hot.

The use of certain vegetables, such as artichokes and eggplants (aubergines) can be traced to a Jewish influence. Before the 16th century artichokes were only grown in Sicily and in Moorish Spain. Venice imported them from the Orient. The knobbly skinned yellow pumpkin which used to be sold, fried or baked, in the city's steets, is part of the traditional menu for Rosh-ha-shan (Jewish New Year) and for the supper which precedes Yom Kippur (the Day of Atonement). Rice pilaf, cooked with a selection of vegetables is derived from the rice dish which the Jews used to prepare on Fridays to eat on Saturday, when they were forbidden to light their fires.

The processing of goose, every part of which is used, without throwing anything away, also comes from the Jewish tradition. The best parts were salted and preserved in the bird's own fat in the neck, then boiled. These were considered a great delicacy. The much-prized goose "hams," were also derived from the Jewish tradition.

As this brief gastronomic review shows, as time passed, Jewish and Venetian cooking mingled and merged, always managing to achieve a perfect harmony between the incomers' customs and the region's indigenous eating habits. This is illustrated by a recipe which typifies this synergy: Frisinal, a sort of macaroni pie encased in puff pastry, which belongs to Judeo-Venetian cuisine. In conformity with the Kosher rule never to mix meat and milk products, there are two versions – one made with cheese and vegetables, and the other with meat gravy and small pieces of meat.

Serves: 6
Preparation: 35 minutes + 12 hours' soaking
Cooking: about 2 hours
Recipe grading: easy

- 1½ cups/300 g dried cranberry or borlotti beans
- 2 tablespoons extra-virgin olive oil
- 1 onion, finely chopped
- 1 clove garlic, finely chopped
- 1 carrot, finely chopped
- 1 stalk celery, finely chopped
- 1 sprig fresh rosemary, finely chopped
- 1¼ cups/150 g finely chopped pancetta or bacon (streaky bacon)
- salt and freshly ground black pepper
- 5 oz/150 g durum wheat dry pasta (tagliatelle, maltagliati)

Suggested wine: a dry rosé
(Lison Pramaggiore Merlot Rosato)

Pasta e fasioi

Pasta and beans

Soak the beans overnight in a large bowl of water. ▪ Drain the beans and transfer to a saucepan with enough unsalted cold water to cover them. Boil gently for just under 2 hours. ▪ When the beans are very tender, do not drain them. Remove one-third with a slotted spoon and purée in a food mill. ▪ Return the purée to the pan and stir. ▪ Heat the oil in a skillet (frying pan) and fry the onion, garlic, carrot, celery, and rosemary with the pancetta until lightly browned. ▪ Stir this mixture into the beans. Season with salt. Bring the beans back to a boil, add the pasta, cook for 5 minutes, then remove from the heat. ▪ Leave the soup to stand for 20 minutes. Quickly reheat and serve with a grinding of pepper and a trickle of oil.

This is one of the most typical dishes of the Veneto region, where superb beans are grown (Lamon are the most famous type). The variety of pasta varies from place to place: in Vicenza broad tagliatelle are used, while in Verona dark, wholewheat bigoli are preferred.

Polenta fasiolada

Polenta with beans and pancetta

Soak the beans overnight in a large bowl of water. ▪ Gently fry the pancetta and the finely chopped onion in a large, heavy-bottomed saucepan. ▪ Add the strained beans, a few fresh sage leaves or a sprig of rosemary, and sufficient cold water to cover the beans (about 1¼ quarts/1.25 liters). Bring to a boil, then cover and simmer gently for 1 hour. ▪ When the beans are nearly done, add salt to taste and, stirring continuously, gradually sprinkle in the polenta. ▪ Cook slowly for 45 minutes, adding a little warm water now and then if necessary. The polenta should be fairly soft, not stiff. ▪ Turn out onto a board or platter and serve.

Serves: 6
Preparation: 20 minutes + 12 hours' soaking
Cooking: 2 hours
Recipe grading: easy

- 1⅓ cups/250 g dried cranberry, borlotti, or pinto beans
- ¾ cup/90 g diced pancetta or fat bacon (fat streaky bacon)
- ½ onion, finely chopped
- fresh sage or rosemary
- salt
- 2⅓ cups/350 g fine ground polenta

Suggested wine: a dry red
(Colli Berici Cabernet)

If there is some left over, cut it into slices about ¾ in/2 cm thick and fry in boiling hot oil until golden brown.

Serves: 6
Preparation: 20 minutes
Cooking: about 1 hour
Recipe grading: easy

- 1 young chicken, weighing about 2¼ lb/1.2 kg
- 2 quarts/2 liters of chicken broth (homemade or bouillon cube)
- 2 onions
- 2 carrots
- 2 stalks celery
- 4 tablespoons extra-virgin olive oil
- scant ½ cup/100 g butter
- 2 cups/400 g Italian Arborio rice
- ½ cup/125 ml dry white wine
- scant 1 cup/100 g freshly grated parmesan cheese
- salt and freshly ground black pepper

Suggested wine: a dry, full-bodied white (Piave Pinot Bianco)

Risotto alla sbirraglia
Chicken risotto

Rinse the chicken inside and out and cut into six pieces. ▪ Bring the broth to a boil with one onion, one carrot, and one stalk celery. ▪ Simmer while you chop the remaining vegetables finely and fry them gently in the oil and half the butter in a large flameproof casserole or saucepan. ▪ Add the chicken and brown lightly. Continue cooking, moistening with some of the chicken broth at intervals, for about 30 minutes or until the chicken is nearly done. ▪ Add the rice and stir. Pour in the wine and cook until it has evaporated. Continue adding more hot broth a little at a time until the rice is tender but is still firm to the bite. ▪ Stir in the remaining butter and season with salt and pepper. Sprinkle with the parmesan and serve.

The name of this recipe must come from the word "sbirri," historically a pejorative word for the police. The ones employed by the Emperor Franz Joseph of Austria are reputed to have been particularly fond of this risotto. Being very sustaining, it can also be served as a main dish. Another version entails taking the chicken flesh off the bone and cutting it into small pieces before cooking; 1 cup/150 g lean veal, cut into small cubes, can also be added.

Serves: 6
Preparation: 10 minutes
Cooking: about 40 minutes
Recipe grading: easy

- 2 lb/1 kg orange-fleshed pumpkin
- scant ½ cup/100 g butter
- 4 tablespoons extra-virgin olive oil
- 2 cups/400 g Italian risotto rice
- ½ cup/125 ml dry white wine
- 2 cups/500 ml broth/stock (homemade or bouillon cube), boiling
- scant 1 cup/100 g freshly grated parmesan cheese
- salt and freshly ground black pepper

Suggested wine: a dry white
(Veneto Pinot Grigio)

Risoto de suca

Pumpkin risotto

Peel the pumpkin and remove the seeds and fibrous matter. Slice thinly. ▪ Heat half the butter and all the oil gently in a heavy-bottomed saucepan. Add the pumpkin slices, then cover tightly and cook slowly until almost tender. ▪ Add the rice, stirring well to flavor the grains. Pour in the wine and stir until the wine has evaporated. Season with salt and pepper. ▪ Begin adding the broth a little at a time and continue cooking over a very low heat until the rice is done but still al dente (tender but still firm to the bite). ▪ The risotto should be moist but not at all sloppy. ▪ Remove from the heat, stir in the remaining butter and the parmesan, and serve.

For added flavor, add a little grated nutmeg, or a dash of cinnamon.

Risoto de branzin

Fish risotto

Remove all the scales from the outside of the fish, eviscerate (gut) it, and wash thoroughly. ▪ Place in a fish kettle or large saucepan. Add enough cold water to cover it and a few black peppercorns. Bring slowly to a boil and then simmer gently for about 10 minutes, or until it is cooked. ▪ Drain the fish and remove its head, bones, and skin. Break up the flesh into small pieces. ▪ Return the head, bones, and skin to the kettle or saucepan. Add the garlic and bay leaf and boil until the liquid has reduced considerably. ▪ Sauté the shallot in the oil and half the butter in a heavy-bottomed saucepan. Add the pieces of fish and the rice. ▪ Pour in a little of the strained fish stock and continue cooking and adding stock until the rice is virtually done. ▪ Add the wine, let it evaporate, then remove from the heat. ▪ Stir in the remaining butter and sprinkle with the parmesan. Serve very hot.

Serves: 6
Preparation: about 30 minutes
Cooking: about 40 minutes
Recipe grading: easy

- 1 sea bass, about 1¾ lb/800 g in weight
- peppercorns
- 1 clove garlic, peeled and whole
- 1 bay leaf
- 1 shallot, finely chopped
- 4 tablespoons extra-virgin olive oil
- generous ⅓ cup/90 g butter
- 2 cups/400 g Italian risotto rice
- ½ cup/125 ml dry white wine
- scant 1 cup/100 g freshly grated parmesan cheese
- salt

Suggested wine: a dry white
(Veneto Pinot Bianco)

Serves: 6
Preparation: about 40 minutes
Cooking: about 1¼ hours
Recipe grading: complicated

- 1¼ lb/625 g shrimp/prawns
- 1 clove garlic, finely chopped
- 1 small onion, finely chopped
- 3 tablespoons sunflower seed oil
- scant ½ cup/100 g butter
- ½ cup/125 ml dry white wine
- salt
- 3 tablespoons all-purpose/plain flour
- 1 cup/250 ml hot milk
- 1 lb/500 g fresh tagliatelle
- scant 1 cup/100 g freshly grated parmesan cheese
- 2 tablespoons finely chopped flat-leaf parsley

Suggested wine: a dry white
(Breganze Pinot Grigio)

Tagliatelle alla buranella

Tagliatelle with shrimp and white wine

Cook the shrimp in 1 quart/1 liter of boiling water for 10 minutes. Remove with a slotted ladle. Use a pair of sharply pointed scissors to cut down the center of their backs. Pull the sides of the shell apart and take out the flesh, keeping it as intact as possible, and set aside. ▪ Return the shells and heads to the broth and continue boiling until it has reduced by two-thirds. ▪ In a skillet (frying pan), fry the garlic and the onion very gently in the oil and 4 tablespoons of the butter. ▪ Add the reserved shrimp flesh. Sprinkle with the wine and cook until it has evaporated. Season with salt. Remove from heat. ▪ Melt the remaining butter in a small saucepan. Stir in the flour and keep stirring to prevent any lumps forming as you add first the hot milk and then the strained hot broth. Continue cooking and stirring for up to 10 minutes, when the sauce should have a thick, glossy texture. ▪ Cook the tagliatelle in plenty of salted, boiling water until they are al dente (tender but firm to the bite). ▪ Drain and add to the skillet. Pour in the sauce and stir gently while cooking briefly over a low heat. Transfer to a heated serving dish. Sprinkle with the parmesan and parsley. ▪ Bake in a preheated oven at 400°F/200°C/gas 6 until a golden brown crust has formed on top. ▪ Serve very hot.

This dish is frequently to be found on the menus of Venetian restaurants. Try adding a few shellfish with the crustaceans, or poached, filleted fish.

Risoto de scampi

Scampi risotto

Bring 1⅓ quarts/1.3 liters of water to a boil in a deep saucepan with the peeled clove of garlic and the bay leaf. Boil for 10 minutes. ▪ Add the scampi and simmer for 10 minutes. Remove the scampi with a slotted ladle and peel them, reserving the flesh. ▪ Return the shells, heads, etc. to the boiling water and boil for 20 minutes. ▪ Heat half the butter and all the oil in a heavy-bottomed saucepan. Fry the shallot gently without coloring. Add the rice and cook for a few minutes, stirring continuously so that it absorbs the flavor. ▪ Sprinkle with the wine and cook until it has evaporated. Season with salt and pepper. ▪ Add the peeled scampi, followed soon afterward by some of the strained broth. Keep adding more broth, a little at a time, as the rice cooks and absorbs it, stirring frequently. The rice should be just tender but still firm to the bite. ▪ Remove from the heat, gently stir in the remaining butter, followed by the parmesan, and serve.

Serves: 6
Preparation: about 50 minutes
Cooking: about 30 minutes
Recipe grading: easy

- 1 clove garlic
- 1 bay leaf
- 1 lb/500 g raw scampi in their shells
- generous ⅓ cup/90 g butter
- 4 tablespoons extra-virgin olive oil
- 1 shallot, finely chopped
- 2 cups/400 g Italian risotto rice
- ½ cup/125 ml dry white wine
- salt and freshly ground black pepper
- scant 1 cup/100 g freshly grated parmesan cheese

Suggested wine: a dry, fruity white (Breganze Vespaiolo Superiore)

Scampi give this gourmet dish a deliciously delicate flavor. For a less refined version you can use any size of shrimp (prawn).

Gnocchi di zucca

Pumpkin dumplings

Serves: 6
Preparation: 15 minutes
Cooking: about 35 minutes
Recipe grading: easy

- 3 lb/1.5 kg piece of pumpkin
- 2 eggs
- 2⅔ cups/400 g unbleached all-purpose/strong, plain flour
- salt
- generous ⅓ cup/90 g butter

Suggested wine: a light, dry white (Gambellara Tocai Bianco)

Peel the pumpkin and scrape away the seeds and fibrous matter. Cut the flesh into fairly large cubes. Place on a baking sheet and bake in a preheated oven at 400°F/200°C/gas 6 for 20 minutes. ▪ Transfer to a bowl and reduce to a smooth purée with a potato masher while still hot. ▪ Stir in the eggs, flour, and a dash of salt. Combine very thoroughly until the mixture is smooth and firm; if necessary, add a little more flour. ▪ Bring plenty of salted water to the boil in a large, wide saucepan. Shape scant tablespoonfuls of the dough into balls the size of a walnut or a little smaller. Drop them into the water a few at a time and cook for 2–3 minutes. Remove with a slotted spoon and transfer to a heated serving dish. Repeat this until you have used up all the gnocchi dough. ▪ Drizzle with melted butter and serve.

Another use for one of the Veneto region's favorite vegetables, these popular pumpkin dumplings are a specialty of the area around Chioggia, and the delta of the River Po. Try sprinkling them with freshly grated parmesan cheese, a dash of cinnamon, and a tablespoonful of sugar just before serving.

Paste conze

Pasta with pancetta, peas, and mushrooms

Fry the onion and parsley gently in the oil in a large skillet (frying pan). ▪ Add the pancetta and fry until lightly browned and crisp on the outside. Add the peas. ▪ Cook for a few minutes while stirring, then pour in the broth and simmer over a low heat for 20 minutes. ▪ Season with salt and pepper and remove from the heat. ▪ Heat half the butter in a separate skillet with a dash of salt. Add the mushrooms a few at a time and stir so that the moisture they produce can evaporate. Cook until tender (this can take up to 20 minutes). ▪ Cook the pasta in a large saucepan of salted, boiling water until it is cooked al dente (tender but firm to the bite). ▪ Drain well and add to the skillet with the pancetta. Stir in the mushrooms and the remaining butter. ▪ Sprinkle with parmesan and serve.

Serves: 6
Preparation: 15 minutes
Cooking: 30–40 minutes
Recipe grading: easy

- 1 onion, thinly sliced
- 2 tablespoons finely chopped parsley
- 3 tablespoons extra-virgin olive oil
- 1 cup/120 g diced pancetta or fatty bacon
- scant 3 cups/400 g hulled (shelled) fresh or frozen peas
- 1 cup/250 ml stock (homemade or bouillon cube)
- generous 1/3 cup/90 g butter
- 10 oz/300 g sliced mushrooms
- 1 lb/500 g pasta (short or long varieties)
- scant 1 cup/100 g freshly grated parmesan cheese
- salt and freshly ground black pepper

Suggested wine: a dry, fruity white (Roero Arneis)

Secondi piatti

Barnyard animals are the most common meat dishes in the Veneto—chicken, geese, turkey, duck—braised in their cooking juices, roasted, or cooked in sweet and sour sauces. During the hunting season, game animals are also served, while variety meats also have a role to play. But it is seafood which most inspires Venetian cooks, who prepare it with simplicity and care, relying on high quality fish and natural flair, rather than complicated procedures or hard-to-find ingredients.

Baccalà mantecato

Creamed stockfish

Place the stockfish in a large saucepan. Add sufficient cold water to completely cover it and place over a moderate heat. When it comes to a boil, turn off the heat. ▪ Leave to stand in the water for 20 minutes and then drain. Remove the skin and take care to remove not only the large bones but all the very small ones as well. ▪ Break up into very small pieces and transfer to a large mixing bowl. Beat vigorously and continuously with a wooden spoon or a balloon whisk as you gradually add the oil in a thin trickle (the method is similar to making mayonnaise). ▪ Keep stirring or beating in the same direction and adding oil until the fish will absorb no more. The mixture should be light and fluffy like a mousse. Add a little salt, if needed, and season generously with pepper. Stir in the garlic and parsley. ▪ Serve cold or at room temperature.

Serves: 6
Preparation: 10 minutes + 20 minutes' standing
Cooking: 10 minutes
Recipe grading: complicated

- ▪ 2 lb/1 kg presoaked stockfish or dried cod
- ▪ about 1¼ cups/310 ml olive oil
- ▪ salt and freshly ground black pepper
- ▪ 1 clove garlic, finely chopped
- ▪ 2 tablespoons finely chopped parsley

Suggested wine: a dry white (Soave Superiore)

This delicately flavored delicious mousse was traditionally served during Lent or on Christmas Eve. If preferred, use a food processor to blend the oil into the fish mixture.

Serves: 6
Preparation: 20 minutes
Cooking: 3¼ hours
Recipe grading: easy

- 1 young, tender turkey, weighing about 4 lb/2 kg, with giblets
- salt and freshly ground black pepper
- 4 tablespoons butter
- ⅔ cup/150 ml extra-virgin olive oil
- 3–4 leaves fresh sage, torn
- 3 whole ripe pomegranates

Suggested wine: a dry red
(Valpolicella Amarone)

Paeta rosta al melagrano
Roast turkey with pomegranate

To prepare the turkey: use a lighted taper to burn off any down and pull out any remaining quill ends. Rinse well inside and out, then dry. Sprinkle the cavity with a little salt and place half the butter inside. Tie up the turkey so that the legs and wings sit snugly against the sides of the bird. ▪ Place the turkey in a fairly deep roasting pan or ovenproof dish. Smear with the remaining butter, drizzle with two-thirds of the oil, and sprinkle with the sage. ▪ Roast in a preheated oven at 350°F/180°C/gas 4 for 3 hours. Baste with its own juices at intervals as it cooks. ▪ Place the seeds of 2 of the pomegranates in a blender and process to obtain a smooth juice. ▪ After the turkey has been in the oven for about 1½ hours, drizzle with half the pomegranate juice. ▪ Rinse and trim the liver (and the gizzard, if wished), then chop coarsely and fry in 1 tablespoon of the oil over a high heat. Add the remaining pomegranate juice, season with salt and pepper, and remove from the heat. ▪ When the turkey is done, cut it into at least 6 pieces. Place in an ovenproof dish and pour the liver and pomegranate sauce over the top. Sprinkle with the seeds of the remaining pomegranate and roast in a preheated oven at 450°F/230°C/gas 8 for 10 minutes before serving.

This is a specialty of Vicenza and makes a perfect fall meal. As a local proverb says: "When November comes and wine is no longer must, the tender little turkey is ready for roasting."

Fegato alla veneziana
Venetian-style liver

Serves: 6
Preparation: 15 minutes
Cooking: 20 minutes
Recipe grading: easy

- 1½ lb/750 g white onions, thinly sliced
- 4 tablespoons butter
- 2 tablespoons extra-virgin olive oil
- 1½ lb/750 g calves' liver, cut into thin strips
- salt and freshly ground black pepper
- 2 tablespoons finely chopped parsley

Suggested wine: a dry, lightly sparkling red (Raboso Veronese)

Place the onions in a very large skillet (frying pan) over a low heat in the butter and oil. Let them sweat gently for 15 minutes, then add the liver. ▪ Cook over a high heat, stirring and turning constantly for 5 minutes at most. ▪ Sprinkle with a little salt just before removing from the heat (or the liver will become tough). ▪ Season with pepper and sprinkle with the parsley. Serve hot.

This is one of the most famous recipes of the Veneto region, in which the slight sweetness of the onion balances the liver's hint of bitterness, combining to make a superb dish. Serve with potato purée.

Pollastra in tecia con funghi

Braised chicken with mushrooms

Serves: 6
Preparation: 20 minutes
Cooking: 40 minutes
Recipe grading: fairly easy

Rinse and dry the chicken and cut into 6–8 pieces. ▪ Sauté the onion, celery, and carrot briefly in a wide skillet (frying pan) in three-quarters of the butter and two-thirds of the oil. ▪ Lightly flour the chicken pieces and add to the skillet. Fry over a higher heat, turning them so that they brown lightly all over. ▪ Add the wine and let it evaporate. Add the cloves, cinnamon, and tomatoes. Season with salt and pepper. ▪ Cook over a moderate heat for about 30 minutes, adding a little hot water if necessary. ▪ Sauté the mushrooms in the remaining oil over a high heat for 10 minutes (less if cultivated mushrooms are used). ▪ Sprinkle with a little salt and stir into the chicken shortly before it is done. ▪ Add the remaining butter and stir until it melts. ▪ Serve hot.

- 1 oven-ready chicken, weighing about 4 lb/2 kg
- 1 small onion, finely chopped
- 1 small stalk celery, finely chopped
- 1 small carrot, finely chopped
- ½ cup/125 g butter
- 3 tablespoons extra-virgin olive oil
- ⅔ cup/100 g all-purpose/plain flour
- 1 cup/250 ml dry white wine
- 3 cloves
- dash of cinnamon
- 1 lb/500 g canned tomatoes, seeds removed
- salt and freshly ground black pepper
- 1 lb/500 g mushrooms (porcini, or your own choice), thinly sliced

Suggested wine: a light, dry white (Piave Chardonnay)

Serve with freshly made polenta.

Porseo al latte

Pork cooked in milk

Tie the pork up as if for roasting. Place in a deep dish or bowl and pour in sufficient wine to completely cover it. Leave to marinate overnight. ▪ Take the pork out of the wine and dry with paper towels. Season with salt and pepper and place in a flameproof casserole with the butter. Brown all over on a fairly high heat. ▪ Add the milk, sage leaves, and rosemary. Cover the casserole with its lid and cook over a low heat for 2 hours. When the pork has only 20 minutes' cooking time left, turn up the heat and cook, uncovered, to reduce the liquid. ▪ Slice the pork and arrange on a serving dish. Spoon some of the cooking liquid over it and serve.

Serves: 6
Preparation: 20 minutes + 12 hours' marinating
Cooking: 2 hours
Recipe grading: easy

- 3 lb/1.5 kg boned rolled leg or loin of pork
- about 1 quart/1 liter dry white wine
- scant ½ cup/100 g butter
- 1 quart/1 liter milk
- 3 leaves fresh sage
- 1 sprig fresh rosemary
- salt and freshly ground black pepper

Suggested wine: a dry, full-bodied red (Piave Cabernet Sauvignon)

A dash of grated nutmeg can be added at the same time as the other seasonings and herbs.

Faraona in peverada

Casseroled guinea fowl

Remove any remaining quill ends and burn off any down with a lighted taper. Rinse and dry the guinea fowl and cut into 6 pieces. ▪ Melt the butter in a flameproof casserole and add half the oil, the pancetta, and then the guinea fowl pieces. Brown all over on a high heat. ▪ Season with salt and pepper. Drizzle with the wine and turn down the heat to low. Cover and leave to cook for 1 hour, turning the pieces at intervals. ▪ Chop the livers together with the soppressa (use another type of fresh Italian sausage if this is not available), the anchovy fillets, the lemon zest (without any of the white pith), and the garlic. Sauté these ingredients gently in the remaining oil, then add the parsley and the lemon juice. ▪ Drizzle with vinegar to taste and add a little salt if wished (the anchovies are salty). Season generously with pepper and draw aside from the heat, by which time this mixture should have cooked for a total time of about 10 minutes. ▪ Serve the guinea fowl very hot, garnished with the "peverada" savory liver mixture.

Serves: 6
Preparation: 20 minutes
Cooking: about 1 hour
Recipe grading: easy

- 1 oven-ready guinea fowl, weighing about 2 lb/1 kg
- 2 tablespoons butter
- scant ½ cup/100 ml extra-virgin olive oil
- ½ cup/60 g diced pancetta
- salt and freshly ground black pepper
- ½ cup/125 ml dry white wine
- scant 1 cup/200 g guinea fowl or chicken livers
- 1 slice *soppressa veneta* (soft, fresh sausage), see method
- 4 anchovy fillets
- zest and juice of 1 lemon, preferably unwaxed
- 1 clove garlic
- 2 tablespoons finely chopped parsley
- 1–2 tablespoons white wine vinegar

Suggested wine: a dry, full-bodied red (Lison Pramaggiore Cabernet)

Guinea fowl has a distinctive taste, somewhat like game birds but more delicate, and is a favorite with the inhabitants of this region. "Peverada" garnish is used for other roast poultry and feathered game. Half an onion can be substituted for the garlic in the mixture; some cooks add finely chopped pickled chilies instead of black pepper.

Serves: 6
Preparation: 20 minutes
Recipe grading: easy

- 1¾ lb/800 g prime beef fillet or tenderloin, sliced wafer-thin
- 4 egg yolks
- 2 teaspoons mustard powder
- juice of ½ lemon
- salt
- 2 cups/500 ml extra-virgin olive oil
- 3 drops Worcestershire sauce
- 1 tablespoon white wine vinegar

Suggested wine: a dry white
(Soave Superiore Classico)

Carpaccio

Raw beef slivers with special dressing

Arrange the slices of beef on a platter, cover with a sheet of plastic wrap (cling film), and place in the refrigerator for 15 minutes before serving while you prepare the dressing. ▪ Mix the egg yolks in a bowl with the mustard powder, lemon juice, and a dash of salt. Beat with a balloon whisk or electric beater as you add the oil in a tiny trickle until the sauce has thickened and you have used most, if not all, the oil. ▪ Add the Worcestershire sauce and vinegar. ▪ Take the beef out of the refrigerator and spoon some of the sauce over it, letting the sauce trickle off a fork in a grid pattern. ▪ Serve at once, accompanied by a salad of mixed salad greens, handing round the remainder of the sauce separately.

According to legend, this dish was invented half a century ago by Giuseppe Cipriani, patron of Harry's Bar in Venice, to tempt the jaded tastebuds of a noble Venetian lady. The beef must be wafer-thin – ask your butcher to slice it for you – and should be served on the same day it is bought. Try serving it with a dressing of extra-virgin olive oil, lemon juice, and freshly ground black pepper; or with 3½ oz/100 g of arugula/rocket (or thinly sliced artichoke hearts) and 7 oz/200 g of parmesan cheese in flakes.

Sardoni alla greca

Baked sardines with garlic and lemon

Carefully remove the scales from the sardines, take off their heads, then cut down the middle of their bellies and eviscerate (gut) them, opening them out flat. ▪ Roll up each fillet, starting with the broader, head end, and arrange them snugly in a single layer in a lightly oiled ovenproof dish. ▪ Sprinkle with salt, oil, and the parsley and garlic which you should chop very finely together. ▪ Drizzle the vinegar and lemon juice over the sardines and bake in a preheated oven at 400°F/200°C/gas 6 for 20 minutes. ▪ Serve hot or at room temperature.

Serves: 6
Preparation: 20 minutes
Cooking: 20 minutes
Recipe grading: easy

- 2 lb/1 kg large (or small) sardines
- salt
- ½ cup/125 ml extra-virgin olive oil
- 2 tablespoons finely chopped flat-leaf parsley
- 1 clove garlic
- ½ cup/125 ml white wine vinegar
- juice of 2 lemons

Suggested wine: a dry white (Croara)

The description "alla greca" – Greek style – may suggest that this is not a native Venetian dish, but it has certainly been popular in Venice for hundreds of years.

Serves: 6
Preparation: 40 minutes
Cooking: about 1¾ hours
Recipe grading: fairly easy

- 1 oven-ready duck, weighing about
  4 lb/2 kg
- ¼ cup/60 g meat from *soppressa veneta*
  sausage (or other Italian sausage)
- scant ½ cup/100 g finely chopped duck
  (or chicken) liver
- ½ cup/60 g freshly grated
  parmesan cheese
- 1 egg
- 2 tablespoons finely chopped parsley
- salt and freshly ground black pepper
- about ½ cup/60 g fine bread crumbs
- scant 2 tablespoons finely chopped
  fresh pork fat
- 1 sprig rosemary
- scant ⅓ cup/70 ml extra-virgin olive oil
- 4 tablespoons butter
- 2 leaves fresh sage

Suggested wine: a dry red
(Piave Raboso)

Anatra ripiena
Stuffed roast duck

Remove any remaining quill ends and burn off any down with a lighted taper; rinse the duck inside and out, then dry. ▪ Place the sausage meat, liver, parmesan, egg, and parsley in a mixing bowl and combine thoroughly. Season with salt and pepper. ▪ Shape into a large rissole which will fit into the duck's cavity and coat it with the bread crumbs. ▪ Sprinkle the duck inside and out with salt and pepper and place the rissole of stuffing in the cavity. Use a trussing needle and kitchen thread to sew up the vent of the bird. Truss the duck by tying the legs to its sides neatly with kitchen string. ▪ Smear the surface of the duck with the pork fat and rosemary. ▪ Transfer to a roasting pan or oval ovenproof dish with the oil, butter, and sage, then roast in a preheated oven at 350°F/180°C/gas 4 for 1¾ hours or until done. ▪ Cut the duck into at least 6 portions and slice the stuffing. Arrange on a serving dish, spoon some of its cooking juices over the top, and serve.

*Ducks are a favorite in the Veneto region
where they live in the lagoons. Duck with
stuffing was the traditional dish served for the
feast of the Redeemer. For a different flavor,
add three finely crumbled amaretti cookies
and 1 cup/60 g fresh bread crumbs soaked in
Marsala wine to the stuffing mixture.*

Petto d'anatra in agrodolce

Duck breast in sweet sour sauce

Rinse the duck breasts and dry them well. Season with salt and pepper. ▪ Melt one-third of the butter in a skillet (frying pan) and fry the duck breasts over a moderate heat for 5–6 minutes each side. Take them out and keep warm. ▪ Spoon off and discard some of the excess fat from the surface of the juices in the skillet. Stir in the spices, sesame seeds, and ginger root. (Use whole dried seeds and cinnamon bark if possible and grind them finely together with a mortar and pestle.) ▪ Add the honey and, after a minute or two, the vinegar. Cook until the latter has evaporated, then add the brown stock. ▪ Reduce this sauce over a high heat to half its original volume. Remove from the heat, then stir in the remaining butter and beat lightly with a fork. ▪ Carve the duck breasts into strips about 1 in/2.5 cm wide and arrange on a serving dish. Spoon the sauce over the top and serve.

Serves: 6
Preparation: 20 minutes
Cooking: 20 minutes
Recipe grading: easy

- 6 duck breasts, weighing about 7 oz/ 200 g each
- salt and freshly ground black pepper
- ½ cup/125 g butter
- ½ teaspoon each fennel, anise, cumin, coriander, cinnamon bark (see method)
- 1 tablespoon sesame seeds
- small piece fresh ginger root, peeled and finely chopped
- 1 tablespoon clear, runny honey
- 3½ cups/800 ml best red wine vinegar
- 1¼ cups/310 ml homemade veal or duck brown stock or meat extract

Suggested wine: a dry red
(Lison Pramaggiore Cabernet)

Duck is usually eaten in the Veneto region over the summer (from July to September) and is often served as the centerpiece of grand meals to celebrate feast days and other special occasions. This recipe, with its wealth of spices and flavors, reflects the influence of oriental and Middle Eastern cooking. Meat extract (Liebig) dissolved in warm water is a good substitute for the classic veal or duck fond brun used by Venetian cooks.

Seafood in Venice

The secret of fish and seafood lies in their being served as soon as possible after leaving the sea. In the Veneto, fresh fish and seafood are caught daily in the lagoon in Venice and along the Adriatic coast. Brought to the local markets in the early morning, by lunchtime they have been converted into a stunning array of mouthwatering dishes. Not surprisingly, locally caught seafood forms the basis of Venetian cuisine. Given the variety and quality of the local product, it is surprising how the Venetians have adopted the northern dried cod or stockfish, for which they have invented a host of recipes. When stockfish made its first appearance in Venice way back in 1432, no one was very enthusiastic about it. However, fresh seafood was not always easily obtainable in inland areas and the strict laws of the Council of Trent, which forbade meat at certain times of the year, soon made stockfish a popular alternative. As it was officially approved by the Church, some of the most appetizing recipes originated in the kitchens of the religious orders. Stockfish Capuchin-Style (see recipe, page 76) is a classic example: in this irresistible dish, stockfish is cooked in milk until soft and velvety, then mixed with garlic and parsley and sweet white raisins (sultanas) and pine nuts. Creamed Stockfish (see recipe, page 57) and Stockfish Vicenza-Style (see recipe, page 75) are two more typical stockfish recipes. There are endless local variations on each.

The word "stockfish" is derived from the Dutch word stok for "pole" and visch for "fish" (literally "pole-fish") and refers to the way the fish are dried. Large cod, caught off the Lofoten Islands in Norway, are eviscerated, beheaded, and hung up by their tails on wooden frames to dry in the open air, until they are completely dehydrated. The most sought after type in Venice (and consequently the most expensive) is called ragno, a corruption of the name of the largest Norwegian exporter, Ragnar. Ragnar stockfish measure up to 32 in/80 cm in length, and are pure white, with lean flesh turning translucent after it has been soaked.

There is nothing more typically Venetian than seafood. In the best restaurants, platters of freshly caught seafood are displayed in special refrigerated window cases to entice customers in for lunch or dinner. Many of the tastiest dishes are only lightly cooked and served with just a dash of olive oil, lemon, garlic, or parsley, relying on the freshness and quality of the seafood to carry them through.

Baccalà alla vicentina
Vicenza-style stockfish

Remove the skin from the fish without breaking up the flesh. Carefully remove all the bones. ▪ Sauté the onions and garlic in scant ½ cup/100 ml of the oil. Add the anchovies and then the parsley. ▪ Taking care to keep the fish in one piece, open out the sides a little and spoon the onion and anchovy mixture into the cavity. Sprinkle with a little of the flour and half the parmesan, and season with salt and pepper. Gently press the fish closed again. ▪ Slice across the length of the fish, cutting it into stuffed steaks 2 in/5 cm thick. Coat these with the remaining flour and parmesan. ▪ Place the steaks snugly next to one another in a heavy-bottomed flameproof casserole which will just accommodate them in one layer. Pour the milk and the remaining oil over them. ▪ Cook over a gentle heat for at least 4 hours; they must not be stirred, but you can shake the dish or pan gently at intervals to prevent the fish sticking. ▪ Serve very hot as soon as they are done or reheat the next day.

Serves: 6
Preparation: 30 minutes
Cooking: 4 hours
Recipe grading: fairly easy

- 2 lb/1 kg pre-soaked stockfish or dried cod preferably from the wider, thicker part
- 1 lb/500 g onions, finely chopped
- 2 cloves garlic, finely chopped
- 2 cups/500 ml extra-virgin olive oil
- 4 salted anchovies, rinsed, boned, and finely chopped (or 8 anchovy fillets)
- 2 tablespoons finely chopped parsley
- ⅔ cup/100 g all-purpose/plain flour
- scant 1 cup/100 g freshly grated parmesan cheese
- 2 cups/500 ml milk
- salt and freshly ground black pepper

Suggested wine: a light, dry red
(Colli Berici Tocai Rosso di Barbarano)

In the Veneto, baccalà *refers to stockfish, dried cod from northern waters which has been preserved by hanging up to dry in the sun, not the salted variety.*

Baccalà alla cappuccina

Capuchin-style stockfish

Serves: 6
Preparation: 20 minutes
Cooking: 40 minutes
Recipe grading: fairly easy

- 1¾ lb/800 g pre-soaked stockfish or dried cod
- ⅔ cup/100 g all-purpose/plain flour
- 1 large Bermuda/Spanish onion, finely chopped
- ½ cup/125 ml extra-virgin olive oil
- 2 tablespoons butter
- 2 bay leaves
- 4 anchovy fillets
- ⅓ cup/60 g seedless white raisins/sultanas, presoaked
- ⅓ cup/60 g pine nuts
- 2–3 teaspoons sugar
- dash of ground cinnamon
- dash of grated nutmeg
- salt and freshly ground black pepper
- about 1 cup/60 g fresh bread crumbs

Suggested wine: a dry white
(Colli Berici Chardonnay)

Cut the stockfish or dried cod into fairly small pieces and remove all the bones. Coat lightly with flour. ▪ Sauté the finely chopped onion in the oil and butter in a flameproof casserole until tender. ▪ Add the fish and pour in sufficient water to cover it. Add the bay leaves, anchovies, white raisins, pine nuts, sugar, cinnamon, and nutmeg. ▪ Simmer over a moderate heat until the fish has absorbed almost all the liquid. Season with salt and pepper. Cover the surface with a sprinkling of bread crumbs. ▪ Bake in a preheated oven at 350°F/180°C/gas 4 until a golden brown crust has formed on top. ▪ Serve hot.

Another version of this recipe calls for the same quantity of stockfish or dried cod, which is poached for 10 minutes, then flaked and mixed with extra-virgin olive oil, finely chopped garlic and parsley, salt, and pepper.

Serves: 6
Preparation: 20 minutes + 24 hours'
marinating
Cooking: 20 minutes
Recipe grading: easy

- 2 lb/1 kg descaled, cleaned, very fresh
  sardines
- ⅔ cup/100 g all-purpose/plain flour
- oil, for frying
- salt
- ½ cup/125 ml extra-virgin olive oil
- 1¾ lb/800 g white onions, thinly sliced
- 1¼ cups/310 ml white wine vinegar

Suggested wine: a dry white
(Lison Pramaggiore Sauvignon)

Sardelle in saor

Sardines in sweet sour marinade

Rinse the eviscerated (gutted) sardines well and dry with paper towels. Dust lightly with flour and then fry them, a few at a time, in plenty of boiling oil. A cast iron skillet (frying pan) is good for this purpose. As you remove each batch from the oil, spread them out on paper towels to drain briefly and sprinkle them lightly on both sides with a little salt. ▪ Remove the skillet from the heat, leave to cool slightly, and then carefully pour off the oil into a heatproof receptacle. ▪ Heat the olive oil in the same skillet and fry the onions gently until pale golden brown. Pour in the vinegar, let it reduce considerably, then remove from the heat. ▪ Arrange the sardines in layers in a deep dish, alternating with the onions and the liquid, making the last layer of onions and the remaining liquid. ▪ Place the dish in a cool place and leave to stand for at least a day before serving.

Simple to prepare, mouthwatering and nutritious, this dish is perfect for a summer dinner. Serve with slices of cold polenta. In the oldest known recipe, pine nuts and soaked, drained seedless white raisins/sultanas are included in the layers of onions.

Rombo ai funghi

Turbot with mushrooms

Eviscerate (gut) the turbot or brill, trim it, and remove its skin (ask your fish vendor to do this for you). Rinse and dry the fish. ▪ Place the oil and one-third of the butter in the bottom of an oval ovenproof dish. Coat the fish lightly all over with flour and place in the dish. Season with salt and pepper. Dot the surface of the fish with one-third of the remaining butter. ▪ Bake in a preheated oven at 400°F/200°C/gas 6 for 10 minutes. ▪ Take the dish out of the oven, then sprinkle the wine over the fish and return to the oven for another 15 minutes. ▪ Sauté the mushrooms over a moderate heat in the remaining butter for 15 minutes. Season with salt and pepper and remove from the heat. ▪ Take the fish out of the oven and transfer to a heated serving platter. Add its cooking liquid to the mushrooms and their juices and reduce over a moderate heat for 5 minutes. ▪ Spoon the mushrooms and liquid over the fish and serve.

Serves: 6
Preparation: 20 minutes
Cooking: 35 minutes
Recipe grading: easy

- 1 turbot or brill, weighing about 4 lb/2 kg
- 2 tablespoons extra-virgin olive oil
- scant ½ cup/100 g butter, cut into small pieces
- ½ cup/75 g all-purpose/plain flour
- salt and freshly ground white pepper
- 1 cup/250 ml Italian Tocai or Pinot Grigio wine
- 10 oz/300 g mushrooms (porcini or another variety), cleaned, trimmed, and thinly sliced

Suggested wine: a dry white (Soave Classico)

The most sought-after fish for this dish is turbot. The flesh is firm and delicate and should never be overcooked.

Serves: 6
Preparation: about 25 minutes
Cooking: 40–45 minutes
Recipe grading: easy

- 2⅓ lb/1.3 kg whole small squid/ cuttlefish
- 1 small onion, finely chopped
- 2 cloves garlic, finely chopped
- ½ cup/125 ml extra-virgin olive oil
- 1 cup/250 ml dry white wine
- salt and freshly ground black pepper

Suggested wine: a dry white
(Bianco di Custoza)

Seppie col nero

Squid in their ink

Clean the squid by gently pulling the tentacles away from each body sac. Remove and discard the quill or bone inside and snip up the center of the sac to open it out; remove the ink sac carefully and reserve. ▪ Wash under cold running water, rubbing away the slime from the inside of the sac and also its very thin purplish outer skin. ▪ Cut the sacs into ½ in/1 cm wide strips. Open 4 or 5 of the ink sacs and pour the ink into a cup. ▪ Fry the onion and garlic together in the oil in a deep, heavy-bottomed saucepan until they are pale golden brown. ▪ Add the squid and cook for a few minutes. Drizzle with the wine and cook until it has evaporated. ▪ Dilute the ink with 2–3 tablespoons of hot water and add to the saucepan. Stir briefly, then cover and simmer over a low heat for 40 minutes. ▪ Stir gently from time to time and moisten with 2–3 tablespoons of hot water if necessary. ▪ Add salt and pepper when the squid are done. ▪ Serve very hot, ideally with a dish of fluffy, freshly made polenta.

The smaller squid or cuttlefish, usually caught in springtime, are the most delicious, but medium-sized specimens are most suited to this recipe, available until late summer.

Caparossoli in cassopipa

Clams baked in wine

Heat the oil and fry the onion until pale golden brown. ▪ Add the clams, followed by the wine and 3–4 tablespoons of hot water. Cover tightly and simmer over a low heat for 15 minutes. ▪ By this time the clams should have opened. Discard any which are still shut. ▪ Sprinkle with parsley and serve.

Serves: 6
Preparation: 20 minutes
Cooking: 15 minutes
Recipe grading: easy

- ½ cup/125 ml extra-virgin olive oil
- 1 onion, finely chopped
- 2⅓ lb/1.3 kg fresh clams in the shell
- 1 cup/250 ml Italian Tocai or Pinot Grigio wine
- 2 tablespoons finely chopped flat-leaf parsley

Suggested wine: a dry white
(Breganze Pinot Grigio)

This dish is best when cooked in an earthenware casserole. For a different taste, try substituting garlic for onion. It should be cooked whole (peeled and slightly crushed) and discarded as soon as it starts to color. You can also prepare a mixed shellfish dish, adding mussels after the clams, followed, if available, by razor shell clams.

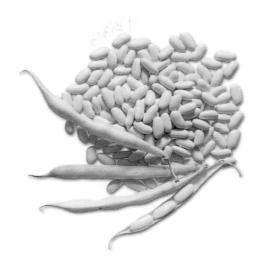

Verdure

The entire Veneto region is renowned for the quantity and quality of its market gardens, although the areas around Mestre and Chioggia are said to produce the best vegetables, thanks to the proximity of the sea. Tender white asparagus and Lamon beans from the Veneto are exported all over Italy. But red Treviso radicchio is the vegetable most clearly associated with the region. Crisp and slightly bitter in taste, radicchio is used in salads, or baked or broiled and served with a drizzle of extra-virgin olive oil and pepper.

Radici di campo fumegà

Wild salad greens with pancetta and onion

Serves: 6
Preparation: 15 minutes
Cooking: 20 minutes
Recipe grading: easy

If you are able to find them, the roots of these wild greens can be scraped clean with a sharp knife under cold running water. Rinse the leaves thoroughly as well; whether wild or cultivated, trim off the fine, stringy ends of the roots. ▪ Fry the pancetta and onion in the oil in a heavy-bottomed skillet (frying pan) or saucepan, then add the radishes (leaves still attached). Sprinkle with a little salt, stir and turn briefly, and then cook gently for about 20 minutes. ▪ Serve hot with boiled or roast meat or poultry.

- 2 lb/1 kg wild salad greens or very fresh small cultivated ones
- ¾ cup/90 g finely diced smoked pancetta
- 1 onion, finely chopped
- 5 tablespoons extra-virgin olive oil
- salt

In the Veneto the slightly bitter wild radish is called "fratocio," gathered in the fields in springtime. Very small cultivated radishes will not need to be cooked for quite so long.

Serves: 6
Preparation: 15 minutes
Cooking: about 25 minutes
Recipe grading: easy

- ½ cup/125 ml extra-virgin olive oil
- 2 tablespoons finely chopped flat-leaf parsley
- 1 clove garlic
- 12 fresh or frozen raw artichoke hearts
- salt and freshly ground black pepper

Suggested wine: a light, dry white
(Soave)

Fondi di carciofo
Artichoke hearts

Pour the oil into a fairly deep, heavy-bottomed skillet (frying pan) or shallow flameproof casserole and add the parsley and garlic, chopped finely together. Sweat these gently rather than fry them. ▪ Add the artichoke hearts, salt, and pepper, and sufficient water to cover the hearts. Cover and cook over a low heat for 10–12 minutes. Remove the lid, then increase the heat and cook for 10 more minutes to allow the cooking liquid to reduce. ▪ Serve hot or at room temperature.

Artichoke hearts are the bases of the flower buds, stripped of all their green, leaf-like bracts and their feathery "choke"; in Venice, the greengrocers sell them ready to cook, kept in cold water acidulated with lemon juice to prevent discoloration. Before adding the water you can drizzle them with ½ cup/125 ml dry white wine and allow it to evaporate. Alternatively, blanch for 15 minutes in boiling salted water acidulated with lemon juice, drain and toss in the garlic, parsley, and oil mixture.

Serves: 6
Preparation: 5 minutes
Cooking: about 35 minutes
Recipe grading: easy

- 2 lb/1 kg medium-sized yellow waxy potatoes
- generous ⅓ cup/90 g butter
- 6 tablespoons extra-virgin olive oil
- 1 onion, thinly sliced
- salt
- 2 tablespoons finely chopped parsley

Suggested wine: a light, dry white
(Lison Pramaggiore Verduzzo)

Patate alla veneziana

Venetian–style potatoes

Wash and peel the potatoes and cut them into small, bite-sized pieces. ▪ Heat the butter and oil in a skillet (frying pan) and fry the onion gently until it is tender and pale golden brown. ▪ Add the potatoes and cook for 30 minutes more, turning frequently. Sprinkle with a little salt only just before serving, otherwise they will become soggy. ▪ Sprinkle with the parsley and serve hot.

Potatoes are the ideal accompaniment for the cooking of this region, with its braised foods and fish dishes. This simple recipe is typical of the unpretentious everyday cooking of ordinary people in the Veneto region.

Fasioi in salsa

Beans with anchovy and garlic dressing

Soak the beans in plenty of cold water overnight. ▪ Drain the beans and place in a saucepan with sufficient fresh cold water to cover. Bring to a boil and simmer gently over a low heat for at least 2 hours; add salt only just before they are done or their skins will toughen. ▪ Fry the garlic and the parsley gently in the oil in a non-metallic saucepan. Discard the garlic when it starts to color. Add the anchovies and cook gently until they have dissolved in the oil. ▪ Add the vinegar and a generous grinding of pepper and simmer, uncovered, for 10 minutes. ▪ Drain the beans when cooked and transfer to a serving dish. Drizzle with the dressing and leave to stand at room temperature for an hour to flavor before serving.

Serves: 6
Preparation: 10 minutes + 12 hours' soaking and 1 hour to flavor
Cooking: 2¼ hours
Recipe grading: easy

- 2 cups/400 g dried beans or 1½ lb/ 750 g if freshly hulled (shelled)
- salt and freshly ground black pepper
- 1 clove garlic, peeled and whole
- 2 tablespoons finely chopped parsley
- generous ¼ cup/70 ml extra-virgin olive oil
- 6 salted anchovies, boned, or 12 anchovy fillets
- 1 cup/250 ml red wine vinegar

Suggested wine: a light, dry white (Piave Chardonnay)

Classic anchovy dressing is ideal with cannellini, cranberry, or borlotti beans.

Radicchio alla trevigiana

Radicchio or red chicory Treviso-style

Serves: 6
Preparation: 10 minutes
Cooking: 20 minutes
Recipe grading: easy

Rinse the radicchio heads and drain thoroughly or shake to get rid of all the water. Trim off the end of the stalk and cut each head lengthwise into 4 long quarters. ▪ Grease a large skillet (frying pan) with a little of the oil and place the radicchio pieces in it in a single layer. Drizzle with the remaining oil and season with salt and pepper. Cook, uncovered, over a gentle heat for 20 minutes, until the radicchio is tender but still crisp. ▪ Serve with various meats and with game.

- ▪ 6 heads Treviso radicchio or red chicory
- ▪ 3–4 tablespoons extra-virgin olive oil
- ▪ salt and freshly ground black pepper

This recipe probably shows Treviso radicchio to its best advantage: tender, flavorsome, but still slightly crunchy. The most traditional way of cooking it is to barbecue it on a grid over embers, turning several times.

The spice trade

Venetian cooking is full of contrasting tastes—sweet, sour, and salty—resulting from the city's centuries-long contact with various Oriental cuisines. By the year 1000, Venice was one of the largest Mediterranean ports and had the greatest volume of maritime trade with the Middle East. It became a major market town, selling on what it imported from the East to the rest of Europe. It dealt in the most disparate merchandise: metals, costly textiles, jewels, perfumes, ivory, incense, but, above all, spices. Venice soon won the monopoly of the trade in spices which were valued in Europe not only for their flavor and medicinal properties but also because of the fascination the West had for Middle Eastern culture which invested food with elements of sensuality and pleasure, in contrast to the spiritual rigor of Christianity. The Serene Republic's ships took on their cargoes from all over the Mediterranean.

From Alexandria, Damascus, and Cairo the vessels returned laden with pepper, nutmeg, cloves, cinnamon, mace, ginger, and cumin. From Crete they brought wine and cheese; from Corinth and Zante, raisins and pine nuts. From the 11th century, the Crusades provided a new opportunity to maximize profits. The Venetians filled their galleys with crusaders and ferried them to Eastern ports to begin their holy wars. Then they loaded them with spices and other cargo before returning home. It was at this time that Venice started to trade in sugar, soon capturing the monopoly, passing laws and entering into agreements with Egypt and Syria where it was produced. Sold on the Rialto Bridge at prohibitive prices, sugar was considered a luxury product. It was used as a therapeutic substance, because of its high energy content.

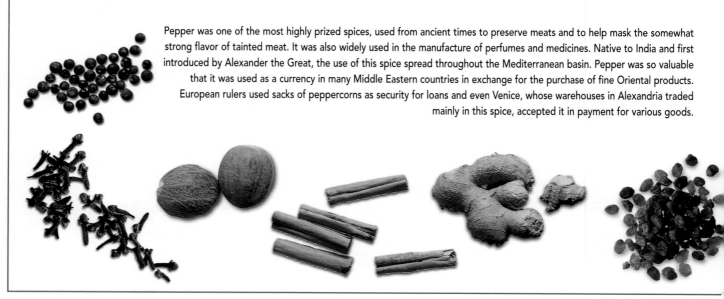

Pepper was one of the most highly prized spices, used from ancient times to preserve meats and to help mask the somewhat strong flavor of tainted meat. It was also widely used in the manufacture of perfumes and medicines. Native to India and first introduced by Alexander the Great, the use of this spice spread throughout the Mediterranean basin. Pepper was so valuable that it was used as a currency in many Middle Eastern countries in exchange for the purchase of fine Oriental products. European rulers used sacks of peppercorns as security for loans and even Venice, whose warehouses in Alexandria traded mainly in this spice, accepted it in payment for various goods.

Sweet and sour, which the Venetians call *dolcegarbo* is recurrent in Venetian cooking. Cinnamon, ginger, nutmeg, cloves, and cumin combined with the sweetish taste of white onions cooked slowly in oil, mellowed by the addition of seedless white raisins (sultanas) or pine nuts; the whole mixture enlivened by the surprising presence of vinegar, with its sharp flavor. Variations on this medley of sweet and sour occur in countless fish, vegetable, and meat dishes.

Paolo Veronese (c.1528–88), born in Verona and part of the Venetian school, is one of Italy's greatest 16th-century artists. His painting, *The Wedding at Cana*, expresses all the fascination the East held for Europeans at the time.

Serves: 6
Preparation: 10 minutes
Cooking: 2 hours
Recipe grading: easy

- Savoy cabbage, weighing about
  4 lb/2 kg
- ¾ cup/90 g finely chopped fresh pork
  fat (replace with butter or extra-virgin
  olive oil, if preferred)
- 1 sprig, rosemary
- 1 clove garlic, whole but lightly crushed
- salt
- scant ½ cup/100 ml dry white wine

Suggested wine: a light, dry white
(Valdadige Pinot Grigio)

Verze sofegae

Braised savoy cabbage

Discard the tougher leaves of the cabbage; then take the rest apart leaf by leaf, cutting out the hard ribs and rinsing. Cut the leaves into thin strips. ▪ Chop the pork fat and rosemary leaves together with a *mezzaluna* (half-moon cutter) or heavy kitchen knife. Fry them briefly in a heavy-bottomed saucepan with the garlic, discarding the latter when it starts to color. ▪ Add the shredded cabbage and a dash of salt and cover. Cook over a low heat, stirring frequently to prevent the cabbage catching and burning, for up to 1 hour. ▪ Add the wine, then cover and continue cooking for another hour. ▪ Serve piping hot.

Braised Savoy cabbage is a classic winter side dish for strongly flavored meat dishes, such as pork or sausages.

Asparagi di Bassano

Asparagus Bassano-style with egg dressing

Use a very sharp, small knife to scrape away the thin outer skin from the lower, slightly woody part of the asparagus stalks. Rinse them thoroughly and tie into bunches with kitchen string. Have the tips arranged level with one another and trim off the ends to make all the stalks the same length. ▪ Place in a tall saucepan of cold salted water, letting the tips protrude above the water level, then cover and bring to a boil. Cook gently for 15 minutes, or until tender (this will depend on the thickness of the asparagus). ▪ Take the asparagus carefully out of the saucepan and refresh by rinsing briefly in a colander under cold running water. This will stop them cooking and keep them an attractive fresh green color. ▪ Mash the eggs in a bowl with a fork, blending in the oil, vinegar, salt, and pepper until smooth. ▪ Arrange the asparagus on a serving dish and spoon the dressing over the tips. Serve.

Serves: 6
Preparation: 15 minutes
Cooking: 15 minutes
Recipe grading: easy

- 3 lb/1.5 kg very fresh, young asparagus
- 4 hard-cooked eggs
- 3 tablespoons extra-virgin olive oil
- 2 tablespoons white wine vinegar
- salt and freshly ground black pepper

Suggested wine: a dry, aromatic white (Veneto Orientale Riesling Italico)

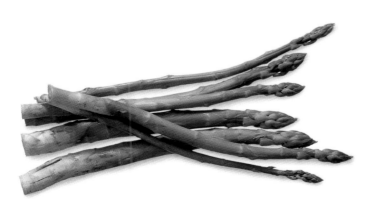

Some cooks add some capers and anchovy fillets, finely chopped together, to the dressing, to give it a sharper taste.

Dolci

Many cakes from the Veneto are rich in spices and dried fruits due to Venice's trading links with the East. They are often made with yellow cornmeal instead of flour. Fritters are also typical of the region—someone once said that the Venetians will add sugar and make fritters out of anything, given half the chance. Made of rice, apples, pumpkin, cream, or sweet bread dough, fritters are traditionally served during Carnivale. Soft and fragrant—Veronese Christmas Cake—is probably the best-known of this region's dessert offerings.

Torta turchesca

Turkish cake

Bring the milk to a boil in a fairly small, nonstick saucepan. ▪ Stir in the sugar, rice, and salt. Cook while stirring continuously for 10 minutes, then drain off any milk which has not been absorbed and transfer the rice to a bowl. ▪ Mix the rice with the almonds, Muscatel raisins, pine nuts, dates, and the eggs and egg yolks. Mix well, adding the citron or rose water. ▪ Transfer the mixture to a turban ring mold previously greased with butter and sprinkled with bread crumbs. ▪ Bake in a preheated oven at 350°F/180°C/gas 4 for 30 minutes, or until lightly browned. ▪ Serve warm.

Serves: 6
Preparation: 20 minutes
Cooking: 40 minutes
Recipe grading: easy

- 1 quart/1 liter milk
- scant $2/3$ cup/125 g sugar
- $1\frac{1}{2}$ cups/300 g uncooked Italian Arborio or round-grain pudding rice
- dash of salt
- $2/3$ cup/100 g very finely chopped almonds
- scant $\frac{1}{2}$ cup/75 g Muscatel raisins, seeded
- generous $\frac{1}{4}$ cup/40 g pine nuts
- 10 dates, preferably fresh, torn into small pieces
- 2 whole eggs + 2 egg yolks
- 1 tablespoon citron water or rose water
- butter and fine bread crumbs for the turban ring mold (tin)

Suggested wine: a sweet, sparkling red (Valpolicella Valpantena Recioto Spumante)

This recipe is a variation on the classic Italian rice cake. Its name and the presence of dates among the ingredients suggests a Middle Eastern influence. For even more color and flavor, try adding a dash each of cinnamon and saffron powder.

Pinza vicentina

Yellow cornmeal and candied fruits cake

Place the almonds in a bowl with the candied peel and cherries, the figs, raisins, fennel seeds, and grappa. Mix well and leave to stand for at least 15 minutes. ▪ Heat the milk to boiling point in a nonstick saucepan or double boiler and then gradually sift the cornmeal and flour into it as you stir continuously with a wooden spoon over a low heat. Cook for 15 minutes, stirring continuously. Add the butter, shortening, sugar, and salt, and cook for 10 minutes more. ▪ Remove from the heat. Add the fruit, nuts, and grappa mixture, and stir well. ▪ Grease a shallow cake or pie pan (tin), 11 in/28 cm in diameter, with butter and dust lightly with flour. Fill with the cake mixture, tapping the bottom on a work surface to make it settle and smoothing the surface. ▪ Bake in a preheated oven at 350°F/180°C/gas 4 for 1 hour, placing a sheet of foil on top of the cake after 30 minutes to prevent it drying out too much. For the same reason it is a good idea to place a small pan of water in the oven at the same time as the cake goes in. ▪ Serve warm.

Serves: 6
Preparation: about 1 hour
Cooking: about 1½ hours
Recipe grading: complicated

- ⅓ cup/60 g almonds, blanched, skinned, and coarsely chopped
- ¼ cup/30 g chopped candied peel and cherries
- 2 tablespoons chopped dried figs
- 2½ tablespoons seedless white raisins/sultanas
- 1 teaspoon fennel seeds
- 6 tablespoons grappa or eau de vie
- 1 quart/1 liter milk
- 2 cups/300 g fine yellow water-ground cornmeal/very fine polenta
- ⅔ cup/100 g all-purpose/ plain flour
- 6 tablespoons butter
- 6 tablespoons shortening/lard
- ½ cup/100 g superfine/caster sugar
- dash of salt

Suggested wine: a medium or sweet white (Soave Recioto Amabile or Dolce)

Yellow cornmeal or polenta is a basic ingredient in Venetian regional cooking, both for sweet and savory dishes. This cake is best eaten on the day it is baked.

Torta sabbiosa

Sandy cake

Serves: 6
Preparation: 30 minutes
Cooking: 45 minutes
Recipe grading: fairly easy

- 1¼ cups/310 g butter
- 1½ cups/300 g superfine/caster sugar
- 3 eggs, separated
- 1 cup/150 g potato flour
- 1 cup/150 g all-purpose/plain flour, sifted
- generous dash of baking powder
- dash of salt

Suggested wine: a sweet, medium or dry sparkling white (Prosecco di Conegliano)

Cut the butter into small pieces and beat vigorously with the sugar in a bowl until it is pale and fluffy (you can use an electric whisk for this). ▪ Beat in the egg yolks, one at a time, making sure each is fully incorporated before adding the next one. ▪ Mix the two types of flour thoroughly with the baking powder. Sift them into the egg, butter, and sugar mixture. Stir until evenly blended. ▪ Whisk the egg whites with a dash of salt until stiff but not dry and fold carefully into the cake mixture with a metal spoon or spatula to avoid crushing the air out of the whites. ▪ Grease the inside of a 10 in/25 cm diameter shallow springform cake pan (tin) with butter and dust with flour. Turn the cake mixture into it, tap the bottom on the work surface, and gently smooth the surface level. ▪ Bake in a preheated oven at 350°F/180°C/gas 4 for 45 minutes. ▪ Cool before serving.

This is a specialty of the Veneto region which has long since become popular throughout Italy. It is soft and crumbly; the secret lies in beating the butter and sugar thoroughly.

Baicoli

Crisp cookies

Serves: 6
Preparation: 40 minutes + 2½ hours' rising
+ 2 days' resting
Cooking: 20 minutes
Recipe grading: fairly easy

- 2⅔ cups/400 g all-purpose/plain flour
- scant 1 cup/200 ml milk
- ½ oz/15 g compressed/fresh yeast
- ¼ cup/50 g superfine/caster sugar
- dash of salt
- 6 tablespoons butter, softened
- 1 egg white, stiffly whisked

Suggested wine: a dry sparkling white
(Prosecco di Conegliano)

Sift a quarter of the flour into a mixing bowl and make a well in the center. ▪ Heat half the milk until it is tepid and mix with the yeast in a small bowl until it has dissolved. ▪ Pour the yeast and milk into the flour and mix to obtain a fairly firm dough. ▪ Knead the dough on a floured work surface, then shape it into ball. Cut a cross shape into the top with a small knife and place in a lightly floured bowl, covered with a cloth, for 30 minutes at warm room temperature. ▪ Sift the remaining flour into a mixing bowl and stir in the sugar and salt. Place the risen dough in the center, then add the butter and egg white. Combine these ingredients together, kneading energetically and adding a little milk to moisten at intervals, using as much as necessary to form a soft dough which holds its shape, similar to bread dough. ▪ Divide the dough into 4 equal portions and shape into small cylinders or sausages. ▪ Transfer to one or more lightly floured cookie (baking) sheets. Cover with a clean cloth and leave to rise for 2 hours. ▪ Bake in a preheated oven at 350°F/180°C/gas 4 for 10 minutes, or until they are golden brown. ▪ Cover and set aside to rest for 2 days. ▪ Slice into wafer thin slices (⅛ in/3 mm thick), then bake in a preheated oven at 325°F/170°C/gas 3 for 10 minutes. Turn after 5 minutes. When cooked, they should be pale golden brown. ▪ Leave to cool and then store in airtight tins.

Carnevale

The incredible variety of feasts and festivals celebrated each year in the Veneto are a tribute to the richness to the region's traditional culture. The city of Venice's festival, Carnevale, held in the early spring each year, is probably the most famous of them all. Over the last twenty years Carnevale has regained all of its former vigour, although much of the popular spirit by which it was once animated has been replaced by the desire to perform for the 500,000 tourists who flock to the celebration each year. Although Carnevale has always been the most popular feast day, there are many other regional celebrations which are well worth a visit. Carnevale in Verona, for example, is celebrated with the local figure of the *"papà gnocco"* (father dumpling). Further north, at Sappada, masked figures celebrate their Carnevale with a traditional costumed race on skis.

Carnevale has been one of the most popular festivals in the Veneto region since the 11th century. Intoxicating and fun-filled, it has also always been an excuse to bend and break the rules of society. The use of masks allows their wearers to exchange roles temporarily or to poke fun at figures of authority without fear of recognition and punishment.

Masks have been worn in Venice for centuries and not just to celebrate Carnevale. During the 14th century, they were worn in many different situations, often where illicit activities such as gambling, duelling, or entering convents dressed as nuns, were involved. Because of this laws were enacted to limit their use to the daytime. A special law in 1608 made them legal only at Carnevale time.

A white mask, known as *La Bauta*, was the most popular mask in the past. Smooth and deathly pale, with just two slits for the eyes, it was fashioned in such a way as to render the wearer's voice unrecognizable. It was worn with a short black cloak and a black three-pointed hat.

Nowadays tradition and innovation mingle on the streets to create a mind-boggling array of costumes and masks that range from the bizarre to the sublime. Wandering the streets of Venice in the final week of the festival is a thrilling experience as masked pieces of cake gather together to form a whole or a team dressed as bricks line up to form a wall.

For centuries, from the 7th of January until Shrove Tuesday, just before Ash Wednesday that signalled the onset of the 40 days of Lent, the city opened itself entirely to the spirit of feast-making. The narrow streets and the canals were full of fantastically masked figures, pharaonic banquests were held in the palaces of the wealthy, and traditional games and dancing were held throughout the city. On the Thursday before Lent crowds of masked revellers paraded through the streets toward Piazza San Marco where ghirlanded bulls were beheaded before the *doge* (city ruler), and the last and most spirited part of the celebrations got underway. Today it is this last week that is still celebrated with real fervour.

Serves: 6
Preparation: 30 minutes + 7½ hours' resting
Cooking: about 50 minutes
Recipe grading: complicated

- 2 cups/300 g all-purpose/plain flour
- ¾ oz/20 g compressed/fresh yeast
- 1 egg + 5 egg yolks
- ⅔ cup/140 g superfine/caster sugar
- 1 tablespoon milk, warmed
- generous ¾ cup/200 g butter, softened
- grated zest of 1 unwaxed lemon
- 4 drops pure vanilla extract/essence
- ½ cup/125 ml light/single cream
- ⅓ cup/50 g confectioners'/icing sugar

Suggested wine: a sweet, medium or dry
sparkling white (Prosecco di Conegliano)

*This is Verona's Christmas cake. It probably
derives from the pan de oro or "golden bread"
of olden days which was served at the very
end of a grand meal, covered with real gold
leaf. Making this distinctive star-shaped,
fluted cake is so complicated and time-
consuming that few are homemade. It is so
typical of the area, however, that it has to
appear in any cookbook about this region.
If you do decide to bake it yourself, you will
find it a satisfying experience.*

Pandoro
Sweet golden yeast cake

Sift 2 tablespoons of the flour into a mixing bowl. Crumble in the yeast and add 1 egg yolk and 1 tablespoon of the sugar. Mix very quickly, adding the milk, to form a soft mixture that can be shaped into a ball. Cover with a cloth and leave to rise for 2 hours at warm room temperature. ▪ Sift half the remaining flour into a mound in a mixing bowl. Place the risen ball of dough in the center with half the remaining sugar, 3 egg yolks, and 3 tablespoons of the butter. Combine all these ingredients quickly and thoroughly. Transfer to a floured work surface and knead to a smooth and elastic dough. Place the dough in a lightly floured bowl, then cover and leave to rise for another 2 hours. ▪ Combine the remaining flour, sugar, egg yolk, and whole egg with the risen dough, kneading energetically. Shape into a ball again, then cover and leave to rise for another 2 hours in the bowl. ▪ Transfer the risen dough to a floured work surface and work in the lemon zest, vanilla, and cream. ▪ Roll the dough out with a floured rolling pin into a rectangle. Place the remaining butter in the center and fold over first one-third of the rectangle, then the other so that you have a 3-layered "sandwich" of dough. Roll it out again and fold again in the same way. Roll it out more gently into a smaller rectangle and leave to rest for 30 minutes. Repeat the last folding and rolling stage once more and leave to rest for a final 30 minutes. ▪ Grease a fluted turban mold (tin) with butter and dust with confectioners' sugar. Add the dough (it should half-fill the mold) and leave to rise until it has reached the top of the mold (about 20 minutes). Bake in a preheated oven at 375°F/190°C/gas 5 for 30 minutes, then turn down to 350°F/180°C/gas 4 and continue baking for a further 20 minutes. ▪ Turn out the cake immediately onto a wire rack; dust liberally with sifted confectioners' sugar and serve.

Serves: 6
Preparation: 20 minutes
Cooking: 25 minutes
Recipe grading: fairly easy

- 5 eggs, separated
- ¾ cup/150 g sugar
- 1¼ cups/200 g all-purpose/plain flour
- 1 quart/1 liter milk, warmed
- grated zest of 1 unwaxed lemon
- 1¾ cups/100 g fresh bread crumbs
- sunflower seed oil, for frying

Suggested wine: a sweet white
(Soave Recioto Dolce)

Crema fritta
Fried sweet egg cream

Place the egg yolks and sugar in a fairly small, heavy-bottomed saucepan (or double boiler) and beat well until they are pale and frothy. ▪ Sift in the flour a little at a time and mix well. Keep stirring as you add the tepid milk and the lemon zest (without any of the white pith). ▪ Place the saucepan over a very low heat and cook the custard while stirring slowly and continuously with a wooden spoon until it becomes very thick. ▪ Turn the custard out onto a lightly oiled marble slab or into a shallow container and leave to cool. ▪ Cut the custard diagonally to produce diamond shapes. Lightly whisk the egg whites. Dip the custard into the egg whites and coat with bread crumbs. ▪ Fry in batches in plenty of very hot oil until they are golden brown. ▪ Drain on kitchen paper and serve hot.

In Venice you can buy this firm egg custard ready made, cold and cut into diamond shapes, all ready to take home to coat and fry. Some dairies also sell it. Serve sprinkled with vanilla-flavored sugar.

Torta fregolotta

Almond cake

Place the almonds in a food processor with 2–3 tablespoons of the sugar and process until they are very finely chopped. ▪ Transfer to a bowl and mix with the flour, salt, and remaining sugar. ▪ Turn this mixture onto a pastry board and heap up in a mound with a well in the center. ▪ Cut the butter into small pieces and add to the almond and flour mixture with the eggs. Use your fingertips to rub them into the dry ingredients, to obtain a mixture that looks like large, crumbly bread crumbs. ▪ Grease a springform pan, 11 in/28 cm in diameter, with butter and dust with flour. Place the mixture in it and press it down gently with your fingertips. Bake in a preheated oven at 350°F/180°C/gas 4 for 40 minutes. ▪ Serve broken into irregular diamond shapes (it is too crumbly to cut it neatly with a knife).

Serves 6
Preparation: 20 minutes
Cooking: 40 minutes
Recipe grading: easy

- 2¼ cups/300 g peeled almonds
- 1¼ cups/250 g sugar
- 2 cups/300 g all-purpose/plain flour
- dash of salt
- generous ¾ cup/200 g butter
- 4 eggs

Suggested wine: a dry sparkling white (Prosecco di Conegliano)

This is a specialty of Castelfranco, in the Treviso area. Its name describes its crumbly texture: fregola *in the Veneto dialect means "crumb." For a slightly different flavor, add the grated zest of 1 lemon to the mixture. There is also a version made without butter, 3–4 tablespoons of light (single) cream being used instead.*

Crostata di ciliege

Cherry pie

Rinse and pit (stone) the cherries. Place them in a bowl with the lemon juice, the first measure of sugar, the cloves, and cinnamon stick. Stir gently and leave to stand and flavor for 2 hours. ▪ To make the pastry: sift the flour into a mixing bowl. Stir in the grated lemon zest and the second measure of sugar. Cut the first measure of butter into small pieces and rub it into the dry ingredients as briefly as possible with your fingertips to obtain a "sandy"-looking texture. ▪ Add the egg yolks and work just enough to combine with the other ingredients. Shape into a ball, wrap in plastic wrap (cling film), and place in the refrigerator. ▪ Spoon the cherry jam into a small saucepan, add the Kirsch and the second measure of butter. Simmer for 5 minutes, then leave to cool. ▪ Divide the pastry dough into two unequal portions (3:1). Roll out the larger one and use it to line a 10 in/25 cm springform pie pan or fairly shallow cake pan (tin) greased with butter and dusted with flour. Leave a narrow border of the pastry lining hanging over the sides. ▪ Spread the cherry jam mixture over the bottom of the pastry and cover with the well-drained cherries. ▪ Roll out the remaining pastry into a sheet and use a fluted pastry wheel to cut it into ½ in/1 cm wide strips. Arrange these on top of the cherries to form a lattice. Fold the overhanging pastry border over the ends of the lattice to form a rolled edging. ▪ Bake in a preheated oven at 375°F/190°C/gas 5 for 40 minutes. ▪ Serve warm rather than hot.

Serves: 6
Preparation: 40 minutes + 2 hours' soaking
Cooking: about 40 minutes
Recipe grading: fairly easy

- 1¾ lb/800 g ripe cherries
- juice of 2 lemons
- generous ½ cup/125 g sugar
- 4 cloves
- 1 cinnamon stick
- 2 cups/300 g all-purpose/plain flour
- grated zest of 1 unwaxed lemon
- ½ cup/100 g sugar
- 2 tablespoons butter
- 3 egg yolks
- 1¼ cups/400 g cherry jam
- 2 tablespoons Kirsch
- ⅔ cup/150 g butter

Suggested wine: a sweet red (Colli di Conegliano Refrontolo Passito Dolce)

This mouthwatering dessert is a specialty of Verona. For a slightly different flavor, try replacing the lemon rind with a few drops of pure vanilla extract (essence).

Coffee

Steaming cups of hot *espresso* have punctuated the daily routine of the people of Venice for centuries. At breakfast time, the fragrant aroma of coffee wafts through the house. During the day, it provides an excellent excuse for a trip to the coffee machine or nearest coffee bar during breaks from work or study. And in the evenings, it is enjoyed while chatting and relaxing in the company of friends

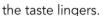

and family. The coffee break has evolved over the years to become almost a rite, always performed in the same way, using the same gestures, seated whenever possible and never alone. The little spoon in the tiny cup, stirring round and round to dissolve the sugar thoroughly, while savoring the aroma that spirals upward. Raised to the lips, it is gone in two or three sips, although the taste lingers.

There are many legends about the origins of coffee; the most well known one concerns the monks of a monastery in the Yemen who were the first to make an infusion with it after they noticed that goats started running around madly after nibbling the leaves and berries of a particular mountain shrub. Legends aside, we do know that coffee was served as a ritual drink in the Yemen by the 14th century. By the end of the 16th century, it was drunk by Muslims throughout the East. In Mecca and Constantinople it was served in meeting places called *kahave-kane*, which earned the disapproval of those in power who regarded them as dens of political conspiracy. News of the drink reached Venice in 1585 in the report of a diplomat, Gianfranco Morosini, in which he referred to the citizens of Constantinople, who drank "a black water, as boiling hot as they can stand it, which is extracted from a seed called *cavèe* and which they say has the virtue of keeping a man awake." Initially used as a medicine in Venice, coffee soon became a popular beverage. It was less expensive than chocolate and its caffeine content was recognized for its energizing properties.

The first café was opened in 1683, in St. Mark's Square. It was followed by countless others, including the Caffè Quadri, opened in 1775 by Giorgio Quadri, where Turkish coffee was served. Soon the coffee house took on a fundamental role in the city's life, as a place where people could relax, but also as a setting for cultural and political meetings. Cafés were for chatting, gambling, and doing business. Carlo Goldoni's play *The Coffee Shop* shows that coffee (both the place and the drink) were an institution in Venice.

Florian's is probably the best known Venetian café. Founded as *Venezia Trionfante* (Venice Triumphant) in 1720 by Floriano Francesconi, it soon became the top café in Venice, and headquarters to the editorial staff of *La Gazzetta Veneta*, one of Europe's first newspapers. Florian's was a meeting place for intellectuals and political agitators, which led to it being closed down in 1796. Restored in 1858, its rooms were decorated with different motifs: one dedicated to the arts and sciences, another to the seasons, a mirrored room, and another given over to portraits of famous people. Over the centuries it has been frequented by many of the most illustrious names in art and literature, Canova, Foscolo, and Byron in the 18th century, and Wagner, Dickens, Proust, and Pirandello in the 19th century.

Serves: 6
Preparation: about 30 minutes
Cooking: about 35 minutes
Recipe grading: fairly easy

Frittelle di zucca

Sweet pumpkin fritters

- 2 lb/1 kg pumpkin
- 1 cup/180 g seedless white raisins/ sultanas, presoaked
- ¼ cup/50 g sugar
- ⅔ cup/100 g all-purpose/plain flour
- 2 teaspoons baking powder
- grated zest of an unwaxed lemon
- dash of salt
- sunflower seed oil, for frying
- sugar, for sprinkling on the fritters

Suggested wine: a medium white
(Soave Recioto Amabile)

Peel the pumpkin and remove the seeds and fibrous matter. Slice the flesh and place in a saucepan with sufficient cold water to cover. ▪ Cook until the flesh is just tender (not too long, about 20 minutes). ▪ Drain well and press in a cloth to absorb any excess moisture. ▪ Place in a bowl, add the drained raisins, the sugar, the flour and baking powder sifted together, the lemon zest, and salt. Mix thoroughly with a spoon and then shape into little balls about the size of a walnut. ▪ Fry in batches in plenty of very hot oil, removing with a slotted spoon when golden brown all over. ▪ Drain on paper towels. ▪ Sprinkle with sugar and serve immediately.

This recipe comes from Venice, where the fritters are usually served during Lent. There is an almost infinite number of variations from all over the Veneto region.

Torta nicolotta

Poor man's cake

Pour the rum into a bowl and add the raisins to soak. ▪ Cut the bread into small pieces and place it in a mixing bowl. ▪ Bring the milk to a boil and add the butter and sugar. Stir briefly and pour over the bread. ▪ When the bread has absorbed all the milk (this will take about 30 minutes), add the lightly beaten eggs, the drained raisins, and the grated lemon zest. ▪ Mix well and transfer to a fairly deep 10 in/25 cm diameter cake pan (tin) greased with butter and sprinkled with bread crumbs. ▪ Bake in a preheated oven at 350°F/180°C/gas 4 for 30 minutes. ▪ Serve hot, warm, or cold.

Serves: 6
Preparation: 20 minutes + 30 minutes' soaking
Cooking: 30 minutes
Recipe grading: easy

- ½ cup/125 ml dark Jamaica rum
- generous 1 cup/200 g seedless white raisins (small, soft golden sultanas)
- 12 oz/350 g stale or 2–3 day-old white bread (traditionally baked)
- 1 quart/1 liter milk
- scant ½ cup/100 g butter
- 1¼ cups/250 g sugar
- 5 eggs
- grated zest of an unwaxed lemon
- butter and fine dry bread crumbs for the cake pan

Suggested wine: a sweet white
(Soave Recioto Dolce)

This cake is named after the nicolotti, *people who used to inhabit the poorest district of Venice, most of whom were beggars.*

Acknowledgments

The Publishers would like to thank Mastrociliegia, Fiesole (Florence) and Bottega della Pasta (Florence) who kindly lent props for photography.

All photos by MARCO LANZA except:

GIUSEPPE CARFAGNA, ROME: COVER; 2, 3, 6, 7, 8, 9, 11, 12, 13, 23TL, 23BL, 24TL, 36, 37, 39, 43TR, 43B, 72, 73BL, 75, 102TL, 104T, 111, 113; Adriano Nardi, Florence: 104B, 105; Overseas, Milan: 22R, 23R; Scala Group, Florence: 93.

ILLUSTRATIONS: IVAN STALIO 42, 60, 112.